WHAT IS THE BOOK OF NUMBERS?

Kids' Guides to God's Word Series

What Is the Book of Genesis?
What Is the Book of Exodus?
What Is the Book of Leviticus?
What Is the Book of Numbers?
What Is the Book of Deuteronomy?
What Is the Book of Joshua?
What Is the Book of Judges?
What Is the Book of Ruth?
What Is the Book of 1 Samuel?
What Is the Book of 2 Samuel?
What Is the Book of 1 Kings?
What Is the Book of 2 Kings?
What Are the Books of 1–2 Chronicles?
What Are the Books of Ezra & Nehemiah?
What Is the Book of Esther?
What Is the Book of Job?
What Is the Book of Psalms?
What Is the Book of Proverbs?
What Is the Book of Ecclesiastes?
What Are the Books of Song of Songs & Lamentations?
What Is the Book of Isaiah?
What Is the Book of Jeremiah?
What Is the Book of Ezekiel?
What Is the Book of Daniel?
What Are the Books of Hosea–Micah?
What Are the Books of Nahum–Malachi?

What Is the Gospel of Matthew?
What Is the Gospel of Mark?
What Is the Gospel of Luke?
What Is the Gospel of John?
What Is the Book of Acts?
What Is the Book of Romans?
What Is the Book of 1 Corinthians?
What Is the Book of 2 Corinthians?
What Is the Book of Galatians?
What Is the Book of Ephesians?
What Is the Book of Philippians?
What Are the Books of Colossians & Philemon?
What Are the Books of 1–2 Thessalonians?
What Are the Books of 1–2 Timothy & Titus?
What Is the Book of Hebrews?
What Is the Book of James?
What Are the Books of 1–2 Peter & Jude?
What Are the Books of 1-3 John?
What Is the Book of Revelation?

What Is the Book of

NUMBERS?

Michael Whitworth

ISBN 978-1-971767-13-0

Published by Start2Finish
Bend, Oregon 97702
start2finish.org

Printed in the United States of America

30 29 28 27 26 1 2 3 4 5

For my daughter Mikaela—

May you always trust God's promises,
even when the journey is harder
and longer than you expected.
Daddy loves you.

CONTENTS

INTRODUCTION

Have you ever been on a road trip that should have taken a few hours but ended up taking all day? Maybe there was construction. Maybe someone insisted on stopping at every gas station. Maybe the GPS led you down a "shortcut" that turned into a dirt road that turned into a dead end that turned into your dad saying words he told you never to repeat. What should have been simple became complicated. What should have been quick became endless.

Now imagine that road trip lasting forty years. That's the book of Numbers. It's the story of a journey that should have taken about two weeks but instead took four decades. Not because the distance was too far. Not because the enemies were too strong. But because the people who were making the trip refused to trust the God who was leading them.

Numbers is one of those books most people skip. It has a reputation for being boring—full of census lists and camping instructions and laws about skin diseases. And honestly? Parts of it are challenging to read. The name "Numbers" comes from the two censuses in the book, and there's a reason most people don't read census reports for fun.

But here's what you'll miss if you skip Numbers: some of the most dramatic stories in the entire Bible. A prophet whose donkey sees an angel he can't see. A bronze snake on a pole that heals everyone who looks at it. The ground opening up and swallowing rebels alive. Water gushing from a rock. And one devastating decision at a place called Kadesh that changed everything for an entire generation.

Numbers isn't boring. It's heartbreaking. It's the story of what happens when people who have seen incredible miracles still refuse to believe. It's the story of a generation that walked out of Egypt in triumph and died in the wilderness in disgrace. And it's the story of a God who remained faithful even when his people weren't.

WHERE WE ARE IN THE STORY

To understand Numbers, you need to know what came before. Genesis told the story of beginnings—creation, the fall, the flood, and then the family of Abraham. God made a promise to Abraham: his descendants would become a great nation, they would bless the whole world, and they would inherit a land of their own. Abraham believed the promise, but he never saw it fulfilled. Neither did his son Isaac or his grandson Jacob. The family grew, but they remained wanderers.

Then came Exodus. Jacob's family (about seventy people) moved to Egypt during a famine. Four hundred years later, they had grown into a nation of millions, but they were slaves. God raised up Moses, sent ten devastating plagues, and led his people out of Egypt through the parted waters of the Red Sea. He brought them to Mount Sinai, gave them his law, and made a covenant with them. They built a tabernacle, a portable tent where God's presence would dwell among them.

Leviticus, the book most people skip even faster than Numbers, explained how sinful people could live in the presence of a holy God. It detailed the sacrificial system, the priesthood, and the purity laws that would make it possible for God to dwell in the midst of his people without destroying them.

And now comes Numbers. The tabernacle is finished. The law has been given. The priests know their jobs. The people are organized, counted, and ready. After nearly a year camped at Mount Sinai, Israel is finally prepared to march toward the land God promised Abraham five hundred years earlier.

The journey from Sinai to Canaan should take about eleven days on foot. It will take them forty years.

WHAT YOU'RE ABOUT TO READ

Numbers covers that entire forty-year period, but it doesn't give equal attention to every part. Think of it as a story with two main acts, separated by a long intermission.

Act One (Chapters 1–14) covers just over a year. Israel prepares to leave Sinai, begins the march toward Canaan, and arrives at the border of the Promised Land. Scouts are sent in. Reports come back. And then disaster. The people refuse to enter the land because they're afraid of the inhabitants. God's response is devastating: that entire generation, everyone twenty years old or older, will die in the wilderness. Only their children will inherit the promise.

The Intermission (Chapters 15–19) covers the next thirty-eight years, but it takes up only five chapters. These are the wilderness years—the long, slow dying of a generation that had seen God's miracles but refused to trust him. The chapters contain laws, rebellions, and provisions for dealing with death and uncleanness. It's a grim section, but it's not meaningless. Even in judgment, God was preparing his people for what would come next.

Act Two (Chapters 20–36) picks up at the end of the forty years. The old generation has died. A new generation has grown up. And now, finally, Israel is ready to approach the Promised Land again—this time from the east, across the Jordan River. These chapters include Moses' own failure (which costs him entry into the land), military victories, a talking donkey, a seductive trap, a second census, and final preparations for entering Canaan.

The book ends with Israel camped on the plains of Moab, looking across the Jordan at the land their parents had been too afraid to enter. They're so close they can almost touch it.

WHAT THIS BOOK IS REALLY ABOUT

Numbers might seem like it's about logistics: counting people, organizing camps, establishing laws. But at its heart, it's about something much more important: faith.

Specifically, it's about what happens when faith fails. The generation that left Egypt had seen things no one else in history had witnessed. They watched the Nile turn to blood. They walked through the Red Sea on dry ground. They ate bread that appeared miraculously every morning. They followed a cloud by day and fire by night. They heard God's voice thunder from a mountain. And still, they didn't trust him.

When they reached the border of Canaan and saw that the inhabitants were powerful, they panicked. They forgot the plagues. They forgot the parted sea. They forgot the daily manna. All they could see were the obstacles in front of them, and they concluded that God couldn't handle it.

That's the tragedy of Numbers. Not that the obstacles were too big, but that the people forgot how big their God was.

But here's the other side of the story: even when Israel's faith failed, God's faithfulness didn't. He disciplined the rebellious generation, but he didn't abandon them. He provided for them in the wilderness. He protected them from enemies. He raised up a new generation to receive what their parents had forfeited. And he kept moving his plan forward—the plan that would eventually bring blessing to the whole world through Abraham's offspring.

Numbers teaches us that our failures don't stop God's purposes. They may delay them. They may bring painful consequences. But God is faithful even when we're not.

A WORD BEFORE WE BEGIN

I should warn you: Numbers contains some difficult material. There's judgment. People die—sometimes suddenly, sometimes in large numbers. God doesn't tolerate rebellion the way we might expect a loving God to do. If you're looking for a book where God is always gentle and affirming, Numbers will challenge you.

There's violence. Israel fights battles. Enemies are defeated. Some passages describe warfare in ways that make modern readers uncomfortable.

There's failure—lots of it. The hero of the story, Moses himself, makes a mistake near the end that costs him entry into the Promised Land. Almost no one comes out of Numbers looking good.

Why does the Bible include all of this? Because it's true. Because God doesn't sugarcoat what happened. Because we need to see both the consequences of unbelief and the persistence of grace. Numbers shows us what we're capable of at our worst, and it shows us what God is like even then.

THE THREAD THAT RUNS THROUGH

As you read Numbers, watch for a pattern. Over and over, the people face a challenge. Over and over, they respond with fear and complaint instead of faith. Over and over, God provides—sometimes through mercy, sometimes through discipline, always with his purposes intact.

And watch for the hints of something greater coming. A prophet will talk about a star rising from Jacob. A bronze serpent lifted up on a pole will save everyone who looks at it. A new leader named Joshua (whose name means "The LORD saves") will emerge to lead the next generation.

Centuries later, Jesus would point to that bronze serpent and say, "Just as Moses lifted up the snake in the wilderness, so the Son of Man must be lifted up, that everyone who believes may have eternal life" (John 3:14–15)

Numbers is pointing somewhere. The whole Bible is pointing somewhere. And that somewhere is a person.

But we're getting ahead of ourselves. First, we need to count some people, organize some tribes, and prepare to march. The Promised Land is waiting.

Turn the page.

1

GETTING READY TO MOVE

In the movie *Up*, the adventure doesn't start when Carl's house lifts off the ground. It starts before that: with the planning, the preparation, the thousands of balloons being carefully inflated and tied. Before the house can fly to Paradise Falls, everything has to be in place. The helium. The ropes. The right number of balloons in the right positions. Skip the preparation, and the house doesn't get off the ground. Or worse, it tips over and crashes.

The same principle shows up everywhere. Before NASA launches a rocket, there are years of calculations, checklists, and test runs. Before a football team takes the field, there are weeks of training camp, playbook memorization, and conditioning. Before a family takes a cross-country road trip, someone has to pack the car, check the tires, plan the route, and make sure they have enough snacks to survive twelve hours in the minivan.

Preparation isn't the exciting part. Nobody makes movies about astronauts filling out paperwork. But preparation is what makes the exciting part possible.

That's what we find at the beginning of Numbers. After everything that happened in Exodus and Leviticus—the plagues, the escape through the Red Sea, the giving of the Law at Mount Sinai, the construction of the tabernacle—Israel is finally ready to move. The Promised Land is waiting. The journey is about to begin.

But first: preparation.

And in this case, preparation means counting people, organizing tribes, assigning jobs, and making sure everyone knows exactly where they're supposed to be and what they're supposed to do. It's not the most thrilling start to a book, but without it, the journey falls apart before it begins.

WHEN AND WHERE WE ARE

The book of Numbers opens with a simple statement that tells us when and where we are: "The LORD spoke to Moses in the tent of meeting in the Desert of Sinai on the first day of the second month of the second year after the Israelites came out of Egypt."

Let's break that down. The Desert of Sinai is where Israel has been camped for almost a year. This is the same wilderness where Moses saw the burning bush, where God gave the Ten Commandments, where the golden calf disaster happened, and where the tabernacle was built. It's not a vacation destination. It's rocks and sand and harsh sun and not much else. But it's where God met his people.

The "tent of meeting" is another name for the tabernacle, that elaborate portable tent described in Exodus where God's presence dwelt among the Israelites. When the text says God spoke to

Moses in the tent of meeting, it means this isn't just good advice Moses came up with. This is God himself giving instructions.

And the date? One month after the tabernacle was set up and almost exactly a year after Israel escaped from Egypt. Think about that. A year ago, these people were slaves making bricks in Egypt. Now they're a nation with their own laws, their own place of worship, and their own relationship with the living God. A lot can change in a year.

But they're not done yet. They're still in the wilderness. The Promised Land is out there, waiting. And between here and there lies a journey that will require organization, discipline, and faith.

God's first instruction? Count everyone.

THE CENSUS: BUILDING AN ARMY

"Take a census of the whole Israelite community by their clans and families, listing every man by name, one by one. You and Aaron are to count according to their divisions all the men in Israel who are twenty years old or more and able to serve in the army."

In the ancient world, censuses had several purposes: taxation, labor projects, military conscription. This one was primarily military. God was building an army.

Now, if you've been paying attention to the story so far, you might find this a little puzzling. God just delivered Israel from the most powerful nation on earth through miracles—plagues that devastated Egypt, a sea that split in half, water from rocks, bread from heaven. If God can do all that, why does he need an army? Can't he just miracle the Canaanites out of the way?

Here's the thing: God almost never works that way. Yes, he does miracles. Yes, he has unlimited power. But he consistently chooses to work through people. He could have teleported Israel to Canaan overnight. Instead, he's going to walk them there, step by step, and he's going to use them—their feet, their hands, their swords—to take possession of the land. The power will come from God, but the action will come from the people.

This is how God still works. He invites us into his plans. He gives us roles to play in his story. Not because he needs us, but because he wants us involved. The census wasn't just practical; it was God saying to every Israelite man: "You matter. You have a part in this. I know your name."

And God did know their names. The census wasn't just about numbers; it was about identity. Each man was counted "by name, one by one." In a nation of hundreds of thousands, every individual mattered.

THE NUMBERS: A NATION ON THE MOVE

The total number from the census was 603,550 men aged twenty and older who could serve in the army. That's a lot of people. If you include women, children, and the elderly, the total population was probably somewhere between two and three million.

Let that sink in. Two to three million people, living in tents, in the middle of a desert, preparing to march to a new homeland. This wasn't a camping trip. It was a mass migration on a scale hard to imagine.

How do you move that many people? How do you keep order? How do you make sure families don't get separated, supplies don't run out, and everyone ends up in the right place?

You organize. You plan. You count.

The census was broken down by tribe—the twelve tribes descended from the twelve sons of Jacob. Each tribe had a designated leader, and each tribe was counted separately. Judah was the largest with 74,600 fighting men. Manasseh was the smallest with 32,200. The numbers varied, but every tribe had a place.

One tribe, however, wasn't counted with the others.

THE LEVITES: A TRIBE SET APART

"The Levites, however, were not counted along with the other Israelites, as the LORD commanded Moses." The Levites were different. They were the tribe of Moses and Aaron, but more importantly, they were the tribe God chose for special service. While the other tribes would form the army, the Levites would care for the tabernacle, God's dwelling place among his people.

Think about the tabernacle for a moment. This wasn't just a tent where people went to pray. This was, according to the Bible, the actual location where God's presence lived on earth. The same God who created the universe, who spoke the stars into existence, who parted the Red Sea—that God was present in a special way in the tabernacle. The innermost room, the Most Holy Place, contained the ark of the covenant, and above that ark was where God's glory dwelt.

That's an awesome thing. And I mean "awesome" in the old sense—full of awe, even terrifying. The presence of God is wonderful, but it's not safe. God is holy, which means he is completely pure, completely set apart from sin. When sinful humans get too close to that holiness without proper preparation, the results can be deadly.

So the Levites served as a buffer. They camped around the tabernacle, between God's dwelling and the rest of the Israelites. Their job was to protect the tabernacle, but also to protect the people from the dangerous holiness at the center of their camp.

"The Levites are to be responsible for the care of the tabernacle of the Testimony. The Israelites are to set up their tents by divisions, each of them in their own camp under their standard. The Levites, however, are to set up their tents around the tabernacle of the Testimony so that my wrath will not fall on the Israelite community."

This might sound harsh. Why would God's presence bring wrath? But the point isn't that God wanted to harm his people, it's that he wanted to live among them even though their sin made that dangerous. The Levites were part of the solution. They made it possible for a holy God to dwell in the midst of an unholy people.

THE CAMP ARRANGEMENT: GOD AT THE CENTER

Numbers 2 describes how the camp was arranged, and it's a remarkable picture. At the center: the tabernacle, the dwelling place of God.

Immediately around the tabernacle: the Levites, arranged by their three main clans (Gershon, Kohath, and Merari), with Moses, Aaron, and the priests on the eastern side—the most important position, closest to the tabernacle entrance.

Beyond the Levites: the twelve tribes, arranged in four groups of three, positioned on the four sides of the camp—east, south, west, and north.

If you looked down from above, you'd see a massive rectangle with God at the center, the Levites forming an inner ring of protection, and the twelve tribes surrounding everything in an outer ring. It was organized, orderly, and deeply symbolic.

Why did the arrangement matter? Because it showed something true about reality: God belongs at the center. Not at the edge. Not as an afterthought. Not as one option among many. The entire nation was literally organized around his presence.

When Israel packed up to march, they did so in this same order. The tribes on the east moved out first, led by Judah. Then the tabernacle was dismantled and carried by the Levites. Then the remaining tribes followed. God's presence moved at the center of the nation wherever they went.

LEVITE RESPONSIBILITIES: EVERY ROLE MATTERS

Numbers 3–4 get into the specific responsibilities of the Levite clans, and honestly, this is where most readers' eyes start to glaze over. Different families were assigned to carry different parts of the tabernacle. The Kohathites handled the most sacred objects: the ark, the table, the lampstand, the altars. The Gershonites carried the curtains and coverings. The Merarites transported the frames, posts, bases, and hardware.

If that sounds like a lot of detail about tent equipment, you're right. But there's something important happening beneath the surface.

Every piece mattered. Even the tent pegs. Even the ropes. The person assigned to carry the crossbars wasn't less important than the person assigned to carry the altar. The whole tabernacle wouldn't work without every piece in place. Everyone had a role, and every role was necessary.

But there were also strict boundaries. The Kohathites carried the sacred objects, but they weren't allowed to touch them or even look at them while they were uncovered. Aaron and his sons (the priests) had to cover everything first. "The Kohathites must not go in to look at the holy things, even for a moment, or they will die."

That sounds extreme to us. But it made a point that Israel needed to understand: God is not to be treated casually. His holiness is real. His presence is a privilege, not a right. Coming near to God is wonderful—and dangerous. Approach with reverence, or don't approach at all.

WHAT THIS MEANS FOR US

So what do we do with four chapters about ancient census records and tent-carrying assignments? Here's what we can take away:

First, preparation matters to God. The exciting part of the story—battles, miracles, entering the Promised Land—was still ahead. But God didn't skip the preparation. He took time to organize his people, count them, assign roles, and establish order. If you're in a season of preparation rather than action, don't despise it. Sometimes the most important work happens before the visible results appear.

Second, everyone has a place. In the census, every man was counted by name. In the camp, every tribe had a position. In the tabernacle service, every Levite clan had specific duties. There were no unimportant people. The guy carrying tent pegs was serving God just as much as the high priest. Whatever your role—whether it seems glamorous or mundane—it matters if you're doing it for God.

Third, God belongs at the center. The whole camp was arranged around the tabernacle. God's presence was literally the thing around which everything else was organized. What would it look like if your life were arranged the same way? Not God as one commitment among many, but God at the center with everything else positioned around him?

Fourth, holiness is serious. The elaborate precautions around the tabernacle remind us that God's presence isn't something to take lightly. Yes, Jesus has opened the way for us to come boldly before God, but "boldly" doesn't mean "casually." We're invited in, but we're invited to approach the Creator of the universe with reverence.

TALKING POINTS

1. **The census counted every person "by name."** Why do you think this detail is included? What does it tell us about how God sees individuals versus crowds?

2. **The Levites were set apart for service at the tabernacle instead of military duty.** What does it mean to be "set apart" for something? Are there things Christians today should be set apart for?

3. **The camp was organized with God's presence at the center.** What are some things that tend to compete for the "center" position in our lives? What would change if God were truly at the center of how we organized our time, priorities, and relationships?

4. **The Kohathites carried the most sacred objects but weren't allowed to touch or even look at them.** What do you think it would be like to have that job—responsible for holy things but never seeing them? What might God be teaching through this arrangement?

5. **These opening chapters of Numbers are full of details that seem tedious to modern readers.** Why do you think God included this kind of material in the Bible? What might we miss if these chapters weren't there?

The preparation was complete. The census was taken. The camp was organized. The Levites knew their assignments. Every tribe knew where to camp and when to march.

Now it was almost time to move. But before they could leave Sinai, there were a few more things to put in order—matters of purity, blessing, and dedication that would prepare the people not just logistically but spiritually for the journey ahead.

The Promised Land was waiting. Turn the page.

2

KEEPING THE CAMP CLEAN

In *Harry Potter and the Sorcerer's Stone*, there's a moment when Harry first arrives at Hogwarts and learns something surprising: you can't just wander anywhere you want. Certain corridors are off-limits. The third-floor corridor on the right-hand side is "out of bounds to everyone who does not wish to die a very painful death." The Forbidden Forest is, well, forbidden. Even the different house dormitories are protected—you need the right password to get past the portrait of the Fat Lady.

Why all the restrictions? Because Hogwarts isn't an ordinary place. It's a school of magic where powerful and dangerous things exist. The restrictions aren't arbitrary rules invented by grumpy teachers. They're protections. Some areas contain things too dangerous for unprepared students. Some places require special access. The boundaries exist because of what Hogwarts *is*.

Israel's camp had similar restrictions, not because of magical creatures, but because of something far more significant: the presence of God himself.

In the last chapter, we saw how the tabernacle sat at the center of the camp, with the Levites surrounding it and the twelve tribes arranged around them. That arrangement wasn't just about organization. It was about the fact that a holy God was living in the middle of an ordinary camp full of ordinary, imperfect people. And when the holy and the unholy get too close without proper precautions, bad things happen.

Numbers 5–6 deal with this reality. How do you keep a camp clean when God lives there? How do you handle situations that threaten the community's purity? And how do ordinary people dedicate themselves to extraordinary holiness?

These chapters might seem like random ancient laws. But look closer, and you'll find they're really about something that matters deeply: what it means to live in the presence of a holy God.

UNCLEANNESS AND LEAVING THE CAMP

Numbers 5 opens with instructions about who had to leave the camp temporarily. Three categories of people were sent outside: those with serious skin diseases, those with certain bodily discharges, and anyone who had touched a dead body.

Before you react with "that's not fair!"—let's understand what's happening here. These weren't punishments for sin. They were responses to what the Bible calls "uncleanness" or "impurity," and that's a concept we need to understand.

In the ancient world, there was a difference between being morally unclean (sinful) and being ritually unclean (impure). Ritual impurity wasn't about being a bad person. It was about being in a state that was incompatible with approaching holy things. Think of it like this: if you've been working in the garden and you're covered in mud, you're not a bad person, but you probably shouldn't sit on your grandmother's white couch. The issue isn't your character; it's your current condition.

Touching a dead body made you ritually unclean. But if your father died, you *should* be there to bury him. That's not sinful; it's honoring your parent. Still, contact with death put you in a state that needed to be addressed before you could approach the living God.

The same was true of certain diseases and bodily conditions. They weren't punishments. They were just part of living in a physical body in a fallen world. But because the holy God dwelt in the camp, people in these states had to step outside temporarily until they could be cleansed and return.

Why did this matter so much? The text explains: "so they will not defile their camp, where I dwell among them." God wasn't being harsh. He was being present. And his presence required boundaries.

THE TEST FOR AN UNFAITHFUL WIFE

The middle section of Numbers 5 addresses a difficult situation: what happens when a husband suspects his wife of being unfaithful, but there's no proof either way?

This is one of those passages that makes modern readers uncomfortable, and honestly, it should be approached carefully. The situation described is a husband consumed by jealousy, suspicious that his wife has been unfaithful. No witnesses exist. No evidence either way. Just suspicion poisoning a marriage.

What were the options in the ancient world? In many surrounding cultures, a suspicious husband could simply punish or divorce his wife based on nothing but his own feelings.

Some societies had "trial by ordeal," such as throwing the accused into a river to see if she drowned or survived.

What Numbers provides is actually more protective than it might first appear. Instead of leaving the wife at the mercy of her husband's jealousy, the case was taken to the tabernacle. Instead of human judgment, the matter was placed in God's hands. The wife stood "before the LORD," and the outcome depended entirely on God's verdict, not human suspicion.

The ritual involved drinking water mixed with dust from the tabernacle floor. If the woman was guilty, physical consequences would follow. If she was innocent, nothing would happen, and she would be cleared completely, with no lasting stain on her reputation.

The point wasn't to give husbands a weapon against their wives. The point was to take a situation that could easily spiral into injustice and put it under God's authority. The husband couldn't just act on jealousy. The wife wasn't condemned by suspicion alone. God himself would judge.

This is still an uncomfortable passage, and I don't pretend otherwise. But in a world where women often had no recourse against false accusations, this law actually provided a form of protection. God, not the jealous husband, had the final word.

THE NAZIRITE VOW: SET APART FOR GOD

Then comes something completely different: the Nazirite vow. The word "Nazirite" means "one who is set apart" or "one who is dedicated." It described ordinary Israelites who chose to dedicate themselves to God in a special way for a specific period of time.

This wasn't required of anyone. It was voluntary. Maybe someone was going through a difficult season and wanted to express extra devotion to God. Maybe they were praying for something important and wanted to mark that season with a special commitment. Maybe they just wanted to draw closer to God in a tangible way. Whatever the reason, the Nazirite vow was a way for regular people to live, for a time, at a higher level of holiness.

Three rules defined the Nazirite: First, no grape products of any kind. Not just wine—nothing from the grapevine at all. No grapes, raisins, grape juice, or even grape seeds. This wasn't about avoiding drunkenness (though that was part of it). Grapes represented the good life in Canaan, the abundant blessing of the land. Giving them up entirely was a way of saying, "For this season, I'm setting aside even good things to focus completely on God."

Second, no cutting hair. The Nazirite's uncut hair was a visible sign of the vow, something everyone could see that marked them as dedicated to God. It was a bit like wearing a uniform. It identified you as someone living under a special commitment.

Third, no contact with dead bodies. Not even for close family members—not even for a parent or sibling. This was actually stricter than the rules for regular priests. Only the high priest was normally held to this standard. It emphasized that during the vow, nothing could come between the Nazirite and their dedication to God.

What's remarkable about the Nazirite vow is who could take it: anyone. You didn't have to be a priest or a Levite. You didn't have to be wealthy or important. Any ordinary Israelite could choose to set themselves apart for God in this way.

This tells us something important: holiness isn't just for religious professionals. God provides ways for ordinary people to draw near to him in extraordinary ways.

THE PRIESTLY BLESSING

Numbers 6 ends with one of the most beautiful passages in the entire Bible: the priestly blessing. God told Moses to tell Aaron and his sons to bless the Israelites with these words: "The LORD bless you and keep you; the LORD make his face shine on you and be gracious to you; the LORD turn his face toward you and give you peace."

Read that again. This is God himself telling the priests what to say over his people. He's not just permitting blessing; he's commanding it. He wants his people blessed.

The imagery is intimate. "Make his face shine on you" pictures someone looking at you with joy and pleasure, like a parent beaming at their child. "Turn his face toward you" means God paying attention, leaning in, not looking away or ignoring you. "Give you peace" translates a Hebrew word that means far more than just absence of conflict. It means wholeness, completeness, everything being right.

And notice: God says that when the priests speak these words, "*I* will bless them." The priests aren't the source of the blessing. God is. The priests are just the ones God chooses to deliver his blessing to his people.

This blessing has been spoken over God's people for more than three thousand years. It was the words Israelite children heard over them. It's the words many churches still use today. It's a reminder that the God who is holy enough to require boundaries is also the God who delights to bless.

WHAT THIS MEANS FOR US

First, living near God requires taking holiness seriously. The rules about uncleanness and purity might seem strange to us, but they taught something vital: you can't casually wander into God's presence as if it doesn't matter. God welcomes us—he wants us near him—but he's not to be taken lightly. Because of Jesus, we now have access to God that the Israelites couldn't imagine. But "access" doesn't mean "casualness." We approach a holy God. That should shape how we come to him.

Second, God cares about justice and truth. The law about the suspicious husband wasn't about controlling women. It was about putting an impossible situation under God's authority. When human wisdom runs out, when there's no evidence, when suspicion is destroying a relationship, God says, "Bring it to me. I'll judge fairly." He still invites us to bring our messes and conflicts to him today.

Third, ordinary people can pursue extraordinary dedication. The Nazirite vow was voluntary and temporary, but it was open to everyone. You don't have to be a preacher or a monk to set aside a season for focused devotion to God. Maybe it's giving up social media for a month to spend more time in prayer. Maybe it's fasting from entertainment to focus on Scripture. God honors the ordinary person who says, "I want to draw closer to you."

Fourth, God delights to bless his people. The priestly blessing isn't reluctant or grudging. God himself commanded it. He wants his face to shine on you. He wants to be gracious to you. He wants you to have peace. Whatever boundaries and requirements exist are because he wants to be near you safely.

TALKING POINTS

1. **The Israelites who were "unclean" had to temporarily leave the camp—not as punishment, but because of God's presence.** How does this change the way you think about the rules in the Old Testament? What were they actually protecting?
2. **The Nazirite vow was voluntary and open to anyone, men or women, rich or poor.** Why do you think God made a way for ordinary people to pursue extraordinary holiness? What might a modern version of that kind of special dedication look like?
3. **The priestly blessing describes God's "face shining" on his people.** What do you think this imagery is meant to communicate about God's attitude toward those who belong to him?
4. **These chapters deal with several uncomfortable realities: disease, death, jealousy, suspicion.** What does it tell us about God that he addresses these messy parts of human life instead of ignoring them?
5. **God commanded the blessing; he wants to bless his people.** How does this affect the way you think about your relationship with him?

The camp was organized. The boundaries were set. The blessing was spoken over God's people. Now came the final preparations before Israel could finally leave Sinai: the dedication of the tabernacle, the celebration of Passover, and the guidance that would lead them through the wilderness.

After nearly a year at the mountain of God, the journey was finally about to begin. Turn the page.

3

FINAL PREPARATIONS AND THE FIRST STEPS

Remember the scene in *The Lord of the Rings: The Fellowship of the Ring* when the fellowship finally leaves Rivendell? For chapters, they'd been preparing—gathering supplies, deciding who would go, making plans, receiving gifts. Elrond gives them counsel. Bilbo gives Frodo his mithril coat and the sword Sting. The elves provide cloaks and rope. Then, at last, the nine companions set out from the safety of the elven refuge into the wild, heading toward Mordor.

That moment works so powerfully because we've been building to it. All the preparation creates tension. When the journey finally begins, we feel the weight of it.

Numbers 7-10 is that moment for Israel. For nearly a year, Israel has been camped at Mount Sinai. They received the Law. They built the tabernacle. They organized the camp. They counted the people. They assigned roles to the Levites. They established rules for purity and dedication. Now, finally, they're about to move.

But before they take a single step toward the Promised Land, there are a few more things to do. The tabernacle needs to be dedicated. The Levites need to be set apart. The Passover needs to be celebrated. And God needs to show them exactly how he'll lead them through the wilderness.

These chapters might feel like the last few items on a checklist before a long trip. But pay attention because what happens here sets the tone for everything that follows.

DEDICATION OFFERINGS FROM THE TRIBES

Numbers 7 is the longest chapter in the entire book—eighty-nine verses. And honestly? It's repetitive. The same list of gifts appears twelve times, once for each tribe.

Here's what happened: When the tabernacle was finally completed and set up, the leaders of each tribe brought offerings to dedicate it. Think of it like a massive housewarming party for God's dwelling place. Each leader brought the same gifts: silver plates, silver bowls, gold dishes filled with incense, bulls, rams, lambs, and goats for various offerings.

So why does the Bible list each tribe's gifts separately instead of just saying "each tribe brought the same thing"? Because each gift mattered individually. When Nahshon of Judah brought his offering on day one, that was Judah's moment to honor God. When Nethanel of Issachar brought identical gifts on day two, that was Issachar's moment. The repetition isn't lazy writing; it's the text's way of saying that every tribe's worship was significant. God noticed each one.

The gifts themselves were practical. The silver plates and bowls would be used for offerings. The animals would become sacrifices. The incense would fill the tabernacle with fragrance. This wasn't giving God things he didn't need. It was providing what his house would require to function. The tribes were being both generous and thoughtful. They understood what the tabernacle needed and gave accordingly.

By the time all twelve tribes had presented their offerings over twelve days, the tabernacle was fully stocked and ready for service. Israel had given overwhelming generosity to the God who had given them everything.

SETTING APART THE LEVITES

Chapter 8 shifts focus to the Levites. We already learned about their role. They were the tribe set apart to serve at the tabernacle instead of going to war with everyone else. But now they needed to be officially dedicated for their work.

The process was elaborate. First, the Levites were purified. Water was sprinkled on them. They shaved their entire bodies, a striking symbol of starting fresh, being made clean. They washed their clothes. Then animals were sacrificed to make atonement for them.

But here's the most interesting part: all the Israelites gathered and placed their hands on the Levites.

What did that mean? When someone placed their hands on a sacrificial animal, it identified that animal as their representative—this animal is standing in for me. When Israel placed their hands on the Levites, they were saying the same thing: these people are standing in for us. The Levites weren't just religious professionals doing a job. They were substitutes, representing the entire nation in service to God.

Remember from Exodus that God had claimed all the firstborn sons of Israel as his own, because he spared them during the final plague in Egypt. The Levites served in place of all those firstborn sons. They were a living, breathing thank-you offering for the salvation God had provided.

This idea of substitution runs through the whole Bible. One stands in for many. The innocent takes the place of the guilty. It's there in the sacrificial system. It's there in the Levites. And ultimately, it points to Jesus, the one who stood in our place, who was our substitute, who did for us what we couldn't do for ourselves.

THE SECOND PASSOVER

Numbers 9 opens with something that might surprise you: a celebration. God commanded Israel to observe the Passover exactly one year after the first Passover in Egypt. That first Passover was the night death passed over the houses marked with lamb's blood, the night Israel was finally set free from slavery. Now, camping at Sinai, they would remember.

This wasn't optional. The Passover wasn't a nice tradition to observe if you felt like it. It was commanded. God's people needed to remember what he had done for them, not just once, but every year, so they would never forget that their freedom came from him.

But a question arose: What about people who were ceremonially unclean at the time of Passover? What if someone had touched a dead body and couldn't participate in the feast? Were they just out of luck?

The answer reveals something beautiful about God. He made a provision. Those who couldn't observe Passover at the regular time could celebrate it one month later instead. They weren't excluded forever—they got a second chance.

This second-chance Passover wasn't for people who just didn't feel like participating. It was for those who genuinely couldn't because of circumstances beyond their control. God's law was firm, but it wasn't heartless. There was room for mercy within the structure.

The passage even addresses foreigners. If someone from another nation wanted to celebrate Passover with Israel, they could under the same rules as everyone else. God's family wasn't closed to outsiders. There was always room for more at the table.

THE CLOUD OF GOD'S PRESENCE

The second half of chapter 9 describes something Israel had seen before but would now depend on constantly: the cloud.

When the tabernacle was set up, the cloud of God's glory descended and covered it. During the day, it looked like a cloud. At night, it looked like fire. This was the visible sign that God was present with his people. He wasn't an invisible, distant deity. He was right there, in the middle of the camp, making his presence known.

But the cloud wasn't just for show. It was for guidance.

When the cloud lifted from the tabernacle, Israel would pack up and march. When the cloud settled, they would stop and camp. It didn't matter if they'd just arrived somewhere or if they'd been there for a month. When the cloud moved, they moved. When it stopped, they stopped. The text emphasizes this over and over: "At the LORD's command they encamped, and at the LORD's command they set out."

This meant Israel couldn't make their own travel plans. They couldn't decide they liked a particular campsite and wanted to stay longer. They couldn't get impatient and decide to move ahead before God was ready. Their entire journey was determined by following the cloud.

Imagine the faith this required. You've unpacked all your belongings, set up your tent, gotten comfortable, and suddenly the cloud lifts. Time to go. Or you've been stuck in a desolate spot for weeks, eager to move on, but the cloud stays put. You wait.

God wasn't just leading Israel somewhere. He was teaching them to follow. He was building the habit of obedience into their daily lives. Every time they moved or stayed in response to the cloud, they were practicing trust.

THE SILVER TRUMPETS

Numbers 10 introduces a new element: silver trumpets. God commanded Moses to make two silver trumpets that would be used to signal the community. Different trumpet calls meant different things. One signal gathered the leaders. Another assembled the whole congregation. Specific patterns told each section of the camp when it was their turn to move out.

This was practical. With millions of people, you needed a way to communicate across the camp. But the trumpets had a deeper purpose too.

The trumpets would be sounded in three main situations: when Israel went to war, when they celebrated their festivals, and when they offered their sacrifices. In war, the trumpet blast was a call for God to remember his people and come to their aid. In worship, it was a joyful announcement of celebration.

The same trumpets that would someday signal battle against enemies were also used to summon the people to praise.

The message? Israel's whole life—war and worship, conflict and celebration—was to be lived in God's presence, under his direction.

THE MARCH BEGINS

Then comes the moment everything has been building toward. "On the twentieth day of the second month of the second year, the cloud lifted from above the tabernacle of the covenant law."

That's it. That's the signal. After nearly a year at Sinai, Israel was moving out.

The text describes the order of march. Judah's division went first, leading the way. Then came the Levites carrying the tabernacle. Then more tribes. Then more Levites with the holy objects. Then the remaining tribes, with Dan's division bringing up the rear. It was orderly, organized, exactly as God had commanded.

Before they left, Moses invited his brother-in-law Hobab to come with them. Hobab wasn't an Israelite; he was from Midian. But Moses urged him to join: "Come with us and we will treat you well, for the LORD has promised good things to Israel."

Hobab initially declined, saying he'd rather go back to his own land and family. But Moses persisted: "Please don't leave us. You know where we should camp in the wilderness, and you can be our eyes." Moses wanted this outsider to share in what God had promised.

We don't know for certain whether Hobab came along, but later passages suggest his descendants did settle with Israel.

Moses' invitation reminds us that God's people were never meant to be an exclusive club. There was always room for those who wanted to join, always an invitation to outsiders to come and share in God's blessings.

MOSES' PRAYERS FOR THE JOURNEY

The chapter ends with a brief, powerful snapshot. Whenever the ark set out, Moses would say: "Rise up, LORD! May your enemies be scattered; may your foes flee before you." And when the ark came to rest, he would say: "Return, LORD, to the countless thousands of Israel."

These weren't magical incantations. They were prayers, acknowledgments that the journey depended entirely on God. When Israel moved, they needed God to go ahead of them and clear the way. When they stopped, they needed God to remain among them.

The adventure was beginning. The preparations were complete. The cloud was moving. And Israel was finally taking their first steps toward the land God had promised them centuries ago.

Everything looked so promising.

WHAT THIS MEANS FOR US

First, generous giving reflects a generous heart. The twelve tribes gave abundantly to dedicate the tabernacle—not because God needed their stuff, but because giving was a way of honoring him. When we give generously to God's work, we're not paying God back for what he's done. We're expressing love for the one who has given us everything.

Second, God provides substitutes. The Levites stood in for Israel. The sacrifices stood in for the Levites. Throughout Scripture, God makes a way for the guilty through the innocent, for the many through the one. This pattern finds its ultimate fulfillment in Jesus, who stood in our place so we could be made right with God.

Third, remembering matters. The Passover wasn't a one-time event to be forgotten. It was an annual celebration designed to remind every generation of what God had done. We too need regular reminders of God's faithfulness: through Scripture, through the Lord's Supper, through gathering with God's people to retell the story.

Fourth, following God requires daily trust. Israel couldn't plan their own route. They had to watch the cloud and respond. Following God isn't a one-time decision; it's a daily practice of paying attention, being willing to move when he says move, and staying put when he says wait.

Fifth, the invitation is always open. Moses invited an outsider to join Israel's journey. God's people have never been a closed group. There's always room for those who want to come. If you know someone who doesn't yet belong to God's family, you can extend the same invitation: "Come with us. God has promised good things."

TALKING POINTS

1. **Numbers 7 lists the same gifts twelve times—once for each tribe.** What do you think this repetition is meant to communicate? Why would each tribe's gift matter individually?

2. **The Israelites placed their hands on the Levites, identifying them as substitutes.** How does the concept of someone standing in your place show up elsewhere in the Bible? What does it mean that Jesus is our substitute?

3. **God provided a "second-chance Passover" for those who couldn't celebrate at the regular time.** What does this tell you about the balance between God's firm commands and his mercy?

4. **Israel had to follow the cloud—moving when it moved, stopping when it stopped.** What would it look like to live with that kind of daily responsiveness to God's leading? What makes it hard to wait when we want to move, or to move when we're comfortable?

5. **Moses invited his non-Israelite brother-in-law to join the journey.** Who in your life might need an invitation to come and see what God is doing?

The cloud was moving. The trumpets were sounding. After months of preparation, Israel was finally on the march toward the Promised Land.

But here's the tragic truth you need to know going in: this journey should have taken weeks. Instead, it would take forty years.

Not because the distance was too far. Not because the enemies were too strong. But because something was about to go terribly, horribly wrong.

The complaining is about to begin. Turn the page.

4

COMPLAINING BEGINS

In the animated movie *The Prince of Egypt*, there's a powerful scene right after Israel crosses the Red Sea. The water crashes down on Pharaoh's army. The people are safe on the other side. And then—celebration. Dancing, singing, joy. Moses' sister Miriam leads the women with tambourines: "There can be miracles when you believe!"

It's a mountaintop moment. Everything feels possible. God has done the impossible. Freedom is real. The future is bright.

But here's what *The Prince of Egypt* doesn't show you, because this is where the movie ends: within days, the celebration stopped. The singing turned to complaining. The people who had just witnessed the most spectacular rescue in history started whining about the food.

That's Numbers 11.

And honestly? It's one of the most frustrating chapters in the Bible. Not because it's hard to understand, but because it's so painfully relatable. The people had everything going for them. God was visibly present with them. They'd seen miracle after miracle. And still—they complained.

If you've ever wondered why God seems so patient with humanity, Numbers 11–12 will show you. If you've ever wondered why he gets angry, these chapters explain that too. And if you've ever caught yourself complaining about something you should be grateful for, you might recognize yourself in these ancient Israelites more than you'd like to admit.

FIRE AT TABERAH

The chapter opens with a disturbing statement: "Now the people complained about their hardships in the hearing of the LORD, and when he heard them his anger was aroused."

Notice: the text doesn't tell us what they were complaining about. Just "hardships." Probably the journey was difficult. The wilderness was uncomfortable. The excitement of leaving Sinai had worn off, and now they were just … walking. Through sand. In the heat. With no idea how long it would take.

So they complained. And God heard.

Fire broke out at the edges of the camp. Some people died. Moses prayed, and the fire stopped. They named the place Taberah, which means "burning." You might think that would be the end of the complaining. It wasn't.

CRAVING MEAT

Almost immediately, the grumbling started again, and this time, it was specific. They wanted meat. "If only we had meat to eat! We remember the fish we ate in Egypt at no cost—also the cucumbers, melons, leeks, onions and garlic. But now we have lost our appetite; we never see anything but this manna!" Read that carefully. They said the fish in Egypt came "at no cost."

At no cost? They were slaves in Egypt. They worked under brutal conditions. Their baby boys were thrown into the Nile. The "cost" of that fish was their freedom, their dignity, and their children's lives.

But memory is selective. When you're unhappy with your current situation, the past starts looking better than it was. Slavery becomes "the good old days" when you're tired of walking through a desert.

And the manna? That miraculous bread from heaven that appeared every morning, that sustained millions of people in a place where nothing grew? They were sick of it. "We never see anything but this manna!"

The text pauses to describe the manna. It was like coriander seed, looked like resin, could be ground or crushed or cooked, tasted like something made with olive oil. It was a daily miracle, appearing with the morning dew. And they despised it.

Here's what the complaining revealed: the people had forgotten what God had done for them. They'd forgotten the slavery. They'd forgotten the plagues. They'd forgotten the parted sea. All they could see was what they didn't have.

Complaining does that. It distorts your vision. It makes the past seem golden, the present seem unbearable, and the future seem hopeless. It turns God's gifts into burdens.

MOSES AT THE BREAKING POINT

The people wailed. Every family, standing at the entrance of their tents, crying out for meat. And Moses heard it all.

Here's where we see something remarkable: Moses himself hit a breaking point. Not in a sinful way but in a human way.

He cried out to God: "Why have you brought this trouble on your servant? What have I done to displease you that you put the burden of all these people on me? Did I conceive all these people? Did I give them birth? Why do you tell me to carry them in my arms, as a nurse carries an infant? I cannot carry all these people by myself; the burden is too heavy for me. If this is how you are going to treat me, please go ahead and kill me."

Moses was exhausted. Leading millions of complaining people through a wilderness had pushed him to the edge. He felt like a parent with a screaming infant who won't stop crying, except there were hundreds of thousands of crying infants, and they never stopped.

This is important: there's a difference between complaining *against* God and lamenting *to* God. The Israelites complained against God—they accused him of being unfaithful, of ruining their lives, of being worse than slavery. But Moses brought his pain *to* God. He was honest about his suffering, but he was talking *with* God, not *about* him. He was still looking to God for help.

That's what lament looks like. It's honest about pain. It doesn't pretend everything is fine. But it keeps the conversation going with God instead of turning away from him.

THE SEVENTY ELDERS

God responded to Moses with grace. He didn't rebuke him for being exhausted. Instead, he provided help. "Bring me seventy of Israel's elders who are known to you as leaders. I will take some of the power of the Spirit that is on you and put it on them. They will share the burden of the people with you so that you will not have to carry it alone."

Leadership wasn't meant to be carried alone. God gave Moses partners: seventy elders who would share the weight. When the Spirit came on these men, they prophesied, demonstrating that God's power was now on them too.

Two of the elders, Eldad and Medad, weren't at the tent with the others. They'd stayed in the camp. But the Spirit rested on them anyway, and they prophesied right where they were.

Joshua, Moses' young assistant, ran to tell Moses. "Moses, my lord, stop them!" Joshua was worried. If other people were prophesying, did that threaten Moses' authority? Did it diminish his importance?

Moses' response reveals his character: "Are you jealous for my sake? I wish that all the LORD's people were prophets and that the LORD would put his Spirit on them!"

Moses didn't care about protecting his status. He didn't need to be the only person with God's Spirit. He wanted *more* people to have it, not fewer. That's the heart of a true leader, someone who wants others to succeed, not someone who hoards power and prestige.

THE QUAIL AND THE PLAGUE

As for the people's demand for meat, God granted it. But not in the way they expected. "You will not eat it for just one day, or two days, or five, ten or twenty days, but for a whole month—until it comes out of your nostrils and you loathe it—because you have rejected the LORD."

Even Moses struggled to believe this was possible. Six hundred thousand men, plus women and children—where would God get enough meat to feed them for a month?

Would they have to slaughter all their livestock? Catch every fish in the sea?

God's reply cuts through the doubt: "Is the LORD's arm too short? Now you will see whether or not what I say will come true." Then the wind blew. Quail, small migratory birds, came in from the sea, driven by the wind. They covered the ground for miles in every direction, piling up several feet deep. Exhausted from their flight, they were easy to catch. The people gathered them frantically, greedily. Everyone collected at least sixty bushels worth.

But before they could even finish eating, before the meat was consumed, a plague struck. Many people died. They named the place Kibroth Hattaavah, which means "graves of craving." God gave them exactly what they asked for. And it destroyed them.

Sometimes the most dangerous thing is getting what you want.

MIRIAM AND AARON CHALLENGE MOSES

You'd think after watching fire consume people for complaining, and after watching others die from their craving, that everyone would learn their lesson. Chapter 12 proves otherwise. This time, the complaint came from inside Moses' own family.

Miriam and Aaron, Moses' sister and brother, started criticizing him. The surface issue was his wife. Moses had married a Cushite woman, likely someone from the region south of Egypt. Miriam and Aaron objected. But the deeper issue was power. "Has the LORD spoken only through Moses?" they asked. "Hasn't he also spoken through us?"

They were prophets too. They were leaders. Why should Moses be treated as more important? Why should he have the unique relationship with God?

The text inserts a note at this point that feels almost like a defense of Moses: "Now Moses was a very humble man, more humble than anyone else on the face of the earth." Moses wasn't self-promoting. He wasn't grasping for power. He didn't demand special treatment. The accusation against him was completely unjust.

And the LORD heard this.

God summoned all three of them to the tent of meeting. He came down in the pillar of cloud and called Aaron and Miriam forward. "Listen to my words: When there is a prophet among you, I, the LORD, reveal myself to them in visions, I speak to them in dreams. But this is not true of my servant Moses; he is faithful in all my house. With him I speak face to face, clearly and not in riddles; he sees the form of the LORD. Why then were you not afraid to speak against my servant Moses?"

God was clear: Moses wasn't just another prophet. His relationship with God was unique. Other prophets received visions and dreams, symbolic messages that needed interpretation. Moses received direct communication. Face to face. Clear, not confusing.

To speak against Moses was to speak against the one God had uniquely chosen and appointed. It was a challenge not just to Moses but to God's authority.

The cloud departed. And Miriam's skin was covered with a disease—white and flaking, like a corpse. She was immediately cut off, unable to remain in the camp due to her condition.

Aaron, horrified, turned to the brother he had just criticized. "Please, my lord, I ask you not to hold against us the sin we have so foolishly committed."

Notice the shift: suddenly it's "my lord." Suddenly Aaron recognizes Moses' position. Suddenly he needs Moses' help.

Moses didn't rub it in. He didn't say "I told you so." He cried out immediately to God: "Please, God, heal her!"

God heard Moses' prayer. Miriam was healed. But she still had to spend seven days outside the camp, bearing the shame of her sin publicly before she could return. The entire nation waited for her.

WHAT THIS MEANS FOR US

First, complaining reveals what we really believe about God. The Israelites' complaints weren't just about food preferences. They were accusations: God had ruined their lives. God wasn't taking care of them. God was worse than slavery. When we complain, we're often saying something about who we think God is, and it usually isn't flattering to him.

Second, there's a difference between complaining and lamenting. The Israelites complained *against* God—accusing him, turning away from him. Moses lamented *to* God, being honest about his pain but still looking to God for help. Lament keeps the conversation going. Complaining shuts it down. God welcomes your honest pain. He doesn't welcome your accusations.

Third, getting what you want isn't always a blessing. The people demanded meat. God gave them meat. And it killed them. Sometimes God's "no" is protection. Sometimes his "not yet" is kindness. The worst thing that could happen might be getting exactly what you're asking for.

Fourth, true leaders don't hoard power. Moses rejoiced when others received God's Spirit. He wanted more people empowered, not fewer. He prayed for the sister who had just attacked him. If you find yourself jealous when others succeed, or protective of your position, or unwilling to help those who've hurt you, pay attention. That's not the heart God is building in his people.

Fifth, challenging God's appointed authority is serious. Miriam and Aaron weren't just criticizing a brother. They were questioning God's arrangement. God takes it seriously when we undermine the leaders he has placed over us. That doesn't mean leaders are always right or can't be questioned. But it does mean we should approach disagreement with humility rather than envy.

TALKING POINTS

1. **The Israelites remembered Egypt as a place where fish was "free"—forgetting they were slaves.** Why do you think we tend to romanticize the past when we're unhappy in the present? How can we guard against this kind of distorted memory?

2. **Moses reached a breaking point and told God, "If this is how you're going to treat me, please kill me."** How is this different from the Israelites' complaining? What makes lament acceptable when complaint isn't?

3. **God gave the people exactly what they asked for (meat for a month) and it became a curse instead of a blessing.**

Can you think of situations where getting what you want could actually harm you? How should this affect the way we pray?

4. **Moses wished that all God's people were prophets. He wasn't threatened by others receiving God's Spirit.** What does this tell us about healthy leadership? Why is it hard for people in leadership to celebrate others' success?

5. **Aaron and Miriam challenged Moses' unique position.** What's the difference between healthy questioning of leaders and the kind of envious challenge that God punished here?

The journey had barely begun, and already everything was falling apart. Complaining. Craving. Jealousy. Death.

But they were so close now. Just ahead lay Canaan—the land God had promised Abraham centuries ago. Scouts would be sent. Reports would return. And Israel would face the moment that would define an entire generation.

What happened next is the turning point of the entire book. Turn the page.

5

THE DISASTER AT KADESH

Have you ever been on a team where one person's fear became contagious? Maybe it was a sports match, and someone on your side started saying, "We can't win this. Look how good they are." And suddenly the whole team's confidence collapsed. Or maybe it was a group project at school, and one person's negativity spread until nobody believed the project could succeed.

Fear is contagious. So is faith. The question is which one spreads.

In the movie *Hoosiers*, a tiny high school basketball team from rural Indiana makes it to the state championship. When they walk into the massive arena for the final game, the players are overwhelmed. The crowd is enormous. The other team looks unstoppable. They're ready to give up before the game even starts.

But their coach doesn't let fear win. He has them measure the basketball hoop. Same height as back home. He has them measure the free-throw line. Same distance. The court is the same size. The rules haven't changed. The only difference is how big the obstacles *look*.

Numbers 13-14 is like that moment—except the Israelites let fear win. And it cost them everything.

This is the hinge point of the entire book. Everything that happens in Numbers flows from what happens here. The decision made at Kadesh turned a journey of weeks into a wandering of forty years. It transformed a generation of conquerors into a generation of corpses. And it all started because ten men looked at giants and forgot about God.

AT THE DOORSTEP OF THE PROMISED LAND

The Israelites had arrived at Kadesh, on the southern border of Canaan. The Promised Land was right there. After centuries of waiting—from Abraham's first hearing the promise to this very moment—Israel was finally at the doorstep.

God told Moses to send scouts into the land. Not to decide whether they should enter; God had already made that clear. The land was theirs to take. The scouts were sent to gather information: What's the land like? How strong are the people? What kind of cities do they have? Bring back some fruit so everyone can see what's waiting for them.

Moses selected twelve men, one leader from each tribe. Among them were Caleb from the tribe of Judah and a man named Hoshea from the tribe of Ephraim. Moses gave Hoshea a new name: Joshua, which means "The LORD saves."

Remember that name. It becomes important later. Joshua is the Hebrew form of the name we know in Greek as "Jesus." Both names mean the same thing: "The LORD saves." Centuries later, another Joshua—Jesus of Nazareth—would lead God's people into a different kind of promised land. The connection isn't accidental.

The twelve scouts traveled through the entire land, from the southern desert all the way to the northern border at Lebo Hamath (about 350 miles). They explored for forty days, moving through every region: the dry Negev in the south, the hill country, the coastal plain, the Jordan valley. They visited Hebron, the ancient city where Abraham, Isaac, and Jacob were buried—a place saturated with memories of God's faithfulness to their ancestors. They saw everything.

And what they saw was remarkable.

When they reached the Valley of Eshkol, they cut down a single cluster of grapes so large that it took two men to carry it on a pole between them. They also gathered pomegranates and figs. The land was exactly what God had promised: fertile, abundant, flowing with milk and honey.

But they also saw something else. The people living in the land were powerful. The cities were fortified with massive walls. Archaeologists tell us some ancient city walls were thirty to fifty feet high and fifteen feet thick. And there were giants. The descendants of Anak lived there, people so large that the scouts felt like grasshoppers in comparison.

The scouts had seen two things: incredible blessing and intimidating obstacles. Now they had to decide which one would define their report.

THE REPORT: SAME FACTS, DIFFERENT FAITH

When the twelve returned to Kadesh, the entire community gathered to hear their report. It started well: "We went into the land to which you sent us, and it does flow with milk and honey! Here is its fruit." They showed the enormous grape cluster, the pomegranates, the figs. The evidence was undeniable. The land was everything God had promised.

Then came the word that changed everything: "But."

"But the people who live there are powerful, and the cities are fortified and very large. We even saw descendants of Anak there." Ten of the twelve scouts let fear shape their report. They described the inhabitants of Canaan as too strong to defeat. The cities were too well-defended. The giants were too terrifying. "We seemed like grasshoppers in our own eyes, and we looked the same to them."

But Caleb interrupted. He silenced the crowd and declared: "We should go up and take possession of the land, for we can certainly do it."

The ten pushed back harder. "We can't attack those people; they are stronger than we are." They spread a bad report through the camp, claiming the land "devours those living in it." They exaggerated the obstacles and minimized the promise.

Notice what was missing from the ten scouts' report: God. They said, "We can't attack those people; they are stronger than *we* are." Not "they are stronger than God." Not "they can resist God's power." Just "we can't do it." They had calculated the odds—their strength against the Canaanites' strength—and concluded the task was impossible. They left the most important factor out of the equation entirely.

Joshua and Caleb saw the same giants. They measured the same walls. They felt just as small. But their equation included a variable the others ignored: "If the LORD is pleased with us, he will lead us into that land." They didn't have more courage than the other ten—they had more faith. They believed that the God who had humbled Egypt would have no trouble with Canaan.

The difference between the two reports wasn't about the facts. It was about whether God belonged in the calculation.

THE REBELLION

The bad report spread through the camp like wildfire. By nightfall, the entire community was weeping. By morning, they were in full rebellion. "If only we had died in Egypt! Or in this wilderness! Why is the LORD bringing us to this land only to let us fall by the sword? Our wives and children will be taken as plunder. Wouldn't it be better for us to go back to Egypt?" Read that again. They said it would be better to return to slavery than to trust God's promise.

This wasn't just fear. This was accusation. They accused God of leading them into a death trap. They accused him of being cruel, of wanting to see their families destroyed. They took the God who had rescued them from slavery, who had parted the sea, who had provided food and water in the wilderness, and called him a murderer.

Then they said to each other: "We should choose a leader and go back to Egypt." They were ready to abandon Moses. They were ready to abandon God's plan entirely. They wanted to reverse everything and return to the place where their baby boys were thrown into the Nile.

Moses and Aaron fell facedown before the assembly. Joshua and Caleb tore their clothes in grief and tried one more time to change the people's minds: "The land we passed through and explored is exceedingly good. If the LORD is pleased with us, he will lead us into that land and will give it to us. Only do not rebel against the LORD. And do not be afraid of the people of the land, because we will devour them. Their protection is gone, but the LORD is with us. Do not be afraid of them."

The crowd's response? They talked about stoning Joshua and Caleb to death.

GOD'S VERDICT AND MOSES' INTERCESSION

Then the glory of the LORD appeared at the tent of meeting. God spoke to Moses: "How long will these people treat me with contempt? How long will they refuse to believe in me, in spite of all the signs I have performed among them?"

God was ready to destroy the entire nation and start over with Moses. He offered to make Moses into a greater nation than Israel. But Moses interceded. He didn't pray for himself. He prayed for God's glory.

His argument was remarkable: "If you destroy this people, the nations will hear about it. They'll say, 'The LORD was not able to bring these people into the land he promised them; so he slaughtered them in the wilderness.' The Egyptians will think you're weak. They'll think your promise failed."

Then Moses appealed to God's character, quoting words God had spoken about himself: "The LORD is slow to anger, abounding in love and forgiving sin and rebellion." Moses was saying: "You've revealed yourself as a God of mercy. Be who you are. Forgive them."

And God did forgive them. "I have forgiven them, as you asked." But forgiveness didn't mean there were no consequences.

FORTY YEARS: THE SENTENCE

God's verdict was devastating: "Not one of those who saw my glory and the signs I performed in Egypt and in the wilderness but who disobeyed me and tested me ten times—not one of them will ever see the land I promised on oath to their ancestors."

The generation that refused to trust God would never enter the Promised Land. They would wander in the wilderness for forty years—one year for each day the scouts explored the land—until every adult who had rebelled was dead. Their children, the very ones they claimed would be "taken as plunder," would be the ones who actually inherited the promise.

Only two adults from that generation would survive to enter Canaan: Joshua and Caleb, the two scouts who trusted God when everyone else gave in to fear. Their faith would be rewarded. Decades later, an eighty-five-year-old Caleb would stand in the Promised Land and say, "Give me this hill country"—including the very region where the giants lived. The man who wasn't afraid at forty wasn't afraid at eighty-five either.

The ten unfaithful scouts died immediately of a plague. Their fear had poisoned an entire generation, and they bore the weight of that responsibility. Words have consequences. The report they spread wasn't just wrong. It was deadly.

When Moses announced God's judgment, the people's response revealed how little they understood. They mourned, yes—but then they said, "Now we are ready to go up to the land the LORD promised us. Surely we have sinned!" They decided to attack Canaan after all. But it was too late. Moses warned them: "Do not go up, because the LORD is not with you. You will be defeated by your enemies."

They went anyway. Without the ark of the covenant. Without Moses. Without God's presence. They charged up the hill in their own strength—and were crushed. The Amalekites and Canaanites drove them back, defeating them completely.

First they refused to go when God said go. Then they went when God said stay. Both were acts of unbelief. Both ended in disaster.

WHAT THIS MEANS FOR US

First, fear and faith are both contagious—choose which one you'll spread. Ten fearful men infected an entire nation. Two faithful men couldn't overcome the negativity. What you say about the challenges you face matters. When you focus on obstacles without God, you spread fear. When you acknowledge obstacles while trusting God, you spread faith.

Second, the size of your obstacles depends on who you compare them to. The giants were enormous compared to the Israelites. But compared to God? The scouts who feared looked at giants and saw their own smallness. The scouts who trusted looked at giants and saw God's greatness. Same facts, completely different conclusions.

Third, unbelief insults God personally. The Israelites' complaint wasn't just a strategic disagreement about military tactics. It was an accusation that God was cruel, unfaithful, and leading them to destruction. When we refuse to trust God's promises, we're not just making a mistake; we're calling him a liar.

Fourth, forgiveness doesn't always mean no consequences. God forgave Israel. He didn't destroy them. The relationship continued. But the generation that rebelled still died in the wilderness. Forgiveness restores relationship; it doesn't always remove consequences.

Fifth, doing the right thing at the wrong time is still disobedience. Israel's attack the morning after God's verdict wasn't faith. It was another form of rebellion. They still weren't listening to God's voice. They were still doing what seemed right in their own eyes. Obedience means following God's timing, not just God's general directions.

TALKING POINTS

1. **The ten scouts and the two scouts saw exactly the same things: the same fruit, the same giants, the same fortified cities.** Why did they reach such different conclusions? What determines whether we interpret challenges through the lens of fear or faith?

2. **The Israelites accused God of wanting to destroy their families, even though he had rescued them from slavery and provided for them in the wilderness.** Why do you think people sometimes blame God for having evil intentions when things get hard?

3. **Moses prayed for God's reputation among the nations rather than for his own advancement.** What does this teach us about what should motivate our prayers?

4. **God forgave the people but still let the natural consequences unfold—that generation would die in the wilderness.** How do you understand the relationship between forgiveness and consequences? Can both be true at the same time?

5. **Israel refused to enter when God said go, then tried to enter when God said stay. Both were failures.** What's the difference between genuine obedience and just doing the right thing at a time that suits us?

The verdict was final. A generation would die in the wilderness. But the story wasn't over. Those forty years of wandering would bring more rebellion, more judgment, and more surprising grace. There would be snakes and water from rocks and a prophet hired to curse Israel who ended up blessing them instead.

And through it all, God would keep his promise. Not because the people deserved it, but because God is faithful even when his people are not.

The wilderness years had begun. Turn the page.

6

THE FALLOUT AND MORE REBELLION

In *The Lion, the Witch and the Wardrobe*, after Aslan is killed on the Stone Table, something unexpected happens. The table cracks. Death itself is broken. And Susan and Lucy, who watched in horror as the White Witch killed the great lion, now watch in amazement as he comes back to life, stronger than before.

But before resurrection comes death. Before hope comes devastation. And before the children defeat the White Witch, there's a long, dark stretch where everything seems lost.

Numbers 15-19 is that kind of section. The disaster at Kadesh has happened. The sentence has been announced. A whole generation will die in the wilderness. And now comes the fallout—the long, painful aftermath of rebellion.

These chapters might seem like a random collection of laws and strange stories: rules about offerings, a man executed for gathering wood, a rebellion that ends with the ground swallowing people alive, and a bizarre ritual involving a red cow. But they're not random at all. Every piece connects to the same question: How can a rebellious people live in the presence of a holy God?

The answer involves both judgment and grace. Lots of both.

HOPE FOR THE FUTURE, CONSEQUENCES FOR THE PRESENT

Numbers 15 begins with something surprising: hope. "When you enter the land I am giving you as a home…" Wait. Hadn't God just said this generation would die in the wilderness? Yes. But God is already looking beyond them to their children. The promise hasn't been cancelled. It's been delayed. The next generation will enter the land. God is already planning for their worship when they get there.

The chapter describes how to bring offerings properly: how much grain and wine should accompany animal sacrifices, making the offerings like complete meals presented to God. These weren't instructions for the condemned generation; they were instructions for the future. God's promise was still alive.

But then the chapter addresses a harder topic: what happens when people sin. The law distinguished between two kinds of sin. Unintentional sins—mistakes made without realizing it—could be atoned for through sacrifice. A person could bring an offering, and the priest would make atonement for them, and they would be forgiven.

But "defiant" sin was different. This wasn't accidentally breaking a rule. This was deliberately rejecting God's authority, knowing full well what you were doing and not caring. The text says such a person "blasphemes the LORD" and must be "cut off from the people."

Then comes an example. A man was found gathering wood on the Sabbath. This might seem like a minor offense, picking up sticks. But the Sabbath wasn't just a day off; it was a sign of Israel's covenant with God. The whole nation had been told repeatedly that no work was to be done on the Sabbath. This man knew the rule. He broke it anyway, openly, in front of witnesses. He was defying God's authority publicly.

The verdict was death.

This sounds harsh to our ears, and honestly, it should make us uncomfortable. But remember the context: Israel had just committed massive rebellion at Kadesh. God had shown extraordinary patience. And now, immediately afterward, someone was publicly breaking God's law as if it didn't matter at all. The message was clear: defiant sin has consequences. God's patience doesn't mean God doesn't care.

The chapter ends with a provision that seems strange but actually reveals God's grace: tassels. God told the Israelites to put tassels with blue cords on the corners of their garments. Every time they got dressed, every time they looked down at their clothes, they would see these tassels and remember: "I belong to God. His commands matter. I am part of his people." It was a visual reminder sewn into daily life. God knew his people would forget. So he gave them something to help them remember.

KORAH'S REBELLION

Chapter 16 records one of the most dramatic rebellions in the entire Bible. A man named Korah, a Levite, gathered 250 community leaders and challenged Moses and Aaron: "You have gone too far! The whole community is holy, every one of them, and the LORD is with them. Why then do you set yourselves above the LORD's assembly?"

On the surface, this sounds almost democratic. Everyone is holy! Why should Moses and Aaron have special authority? But Korah's argument was deeply flawed. Yes, all Israel was called to be holy. But God had specifically appointed Moses as leader and Aaron as high priest. Korah wasn't challenging Moses and Aaron—he was challenging God's arrangement.

Joined with Korah were Dathan and Abiram, men from the tribe of Reuben. When Moses summoned them, they refused to come. Their response dripped with contempt: "Isn't it enough that you have brought us up out of a land flowing with milk and honey to kill us in the wilderness? And now you also want to lord it over us?"

Did you catch that? They called Egypt—the place of slavery—"a land flowing with milk and honey." They used the exact words God had used to describe the Promised Land and applied them to Egypt instead. They were completely turning reality upside down.

Moses proposed a test. Korah and his followers would bring censers with incense before the Lord. Aaron would do the same. And God himself would show who truly belonged to him.

This was a dangerous test. Offering incense was the exclusive job of the priests. When Aaron's own sons Nadab and Abihu had offered incense improperly, they died instantly. Now 250 men who weren't priests at all would attempt the same task. They were betting their lives that they were right and Moses was wrong.

The next day, they gathered. The whole community assembled to watch. And God's glory appeared. God told Moses and Aaron to separate themselves from the congregation so he could destroy everyone instantly. But Moses and Aaron fell facedown and interceded: "O God, will you be angry with the entire assembly when only one man sins?" God relented—partially. He told the people to move away from the tents of Korah, Dathan, and Abiram.

Then Moses spoke: "This is how you will know that the LORD has sent me: If these men die a natural death, then the LORD has not sent me. But if the LORD brings about something totally new, and the earth opens its mouth and swallows them, then you will know that these men have treated the LORD with contempt."

The moment he finished speaking, the ground split open. Korah, Dathan, and Abiram—along with their households and possessions—fell into the crack. The earth closed over them. They were gone. Then fire came from the Lord and consumed the 250 men offering incense.

You would think this would end the rebellion. It didn't. The very next day, the whole community grumbled against Moses and Aaron: "You have killed the LORD's people!" The LORD's people? These were the rebels who had just been judged! Yet the community blamed Moses and Aaron for the deaths, as if they had somehow caused the earthquake and fire.

God's glory appeared again. A plague broke out. Moses told Aaron to take his censer, put incense on it, and run into the midst of the assembly to make atonement for them. Aaron obeyed, and the plague stopped. But 14,700 people had already died.

Aaron stood between the living and the dead, his incense burning, making atonement. It's a powerful image: the high priest running toward dying people to save them, standing in the gap between judgment and mercy.

AARON'S STAFF

After this catastrophe, God provided visible proof of Aaron's legitimate priesthood. Each tribal leader brought a staff with his name written on it. The staffs were placed in the tabernacle overnight. In the morning, Aaron's staff had not only sprouted—it had budded, blossomed, and produced almonds. Life from a dead stick.

The message was unmistakable: God had chosen Aaron. This wasn't about Moses and Aaron grabbing power; it was about God's appointment. The sprouted staff was kept as a permanent reminder to prevent future rebellions.

Chapter 18 then clarifies the roles and responsibilities of priests and Levites. After the chaos of Korah's rebellion (where Levites had tried to take priestly roles), God made the distinctions crystal clear. Priests served at the altar. Levites assisted but didn't perform sacrifices. Each group had specific duties, and crossing those boundaries meant death.

The chapter also addressed how priests and Levites would be supported. Since they didn't receive land like the other tribes, they would receive portions of the offerings and tithes the people brought. God himself was their inheritance.

THE RED HEIFER: CLEANSING FROM DEATH

Chapter 19 introduces one of the strangest rituals in the entire Bible: the red heifer. A red cow, completely without defect and never yoked for work, was to be slaughtered outside the camp.

It was burned completely—hide, flesh, blood, everything—along with cedar wood, hyssop, and scarlet wool. The ashes were collected and kept outside the camp.

Why outside the camp? Because this wasn't an ordinary sacrifice. The whole point was to deal with defilement, with contamination, with the effects of death. It had to happen outside the boundaries of the community.

What were these ashes for? Cleansing from death. Whenever someone touched a dead body—which happened often, since people die—they became ritually unclean. They couldn't enter the tabernacle or participate in community worship for seven days. This wasn't punishment for doing something wrong. Burying your relatives was the right thing to do. But contact with death created a barrier between you and the holy God of life.

To be cleansed, the ashes of the red heifer were mixed with fresh water, and this "water of cleansing" was sprinkled on the unclean person on the third and seventh days. Then they bathed, washed their clothes, and were clean again.

The text warns that anyone who refused this cleansing, who stayed unclean deliberately, would be "cut off" from the community. It wasn't optional. God had provided a way to be cleansed; refusing to use it was rejecting God's provision.

Why was this necessary? Because death and the holy God of life don't mix. Touching a corpse was unavoidable. You had to bury your dead relatives. But it created a barrier between you and God's presence that needed to be addressed.

Here's what makes the red heifer ritual remarkable: it was free. Normally, a person who became unclean had to bring their own sacrifice. But if every family member who helped bury a loved one had to bring a sacrifice, entire families would go broke after a funeral. God provided a community solution. The ashes were prepared in advance and available for everyone. All you had to do was use them.

The author of Hebrews would later point to this ritual and say: if the ashes of a heifer could make someone outwardly clean, "how much more will the blood of Christ, who through the eternal Spirit offered himself unblemished to God, cleanse our consciences from acts that lead to death" (Hebrews 9:13–14).

The red heifer was a shadow pointing to something greater.

WHAT THIS MEANS FOR US

First, judgment doesn't cancel God's promises; it delays them. The rebellious generation would die, but their children would inherit the land. When we face consequences for our failures, we shouldn't assume God's plans for us are finished. He is a God of second generations, of new starts, of purposes that outlast our mistakes.

Second, defiant sin is different from struggling sin. Everyone struggles with sin. We all fail, sometimes repeatedly. That's not what "defiant sin" means. Defiant sin is deliberately rejecting God's authority, not because you're weak, but because you don't care. It's the difference between falling down and walking away. God has patience for stumbling people. He has judgment for people who shake their fist at him and choose rebellion.

Third, challenging God's appointed leaders is serious. Korah's rebellion wasn't about personality conflicts or management style. He was rejecting God's arrangement. This doesn't mean leaders can't be questioned or that they're always right. But when we challenge authority in the church, we should do so humbly, recognizing that some patterns of leadership come from God himself.

Fourth, intercessors stand between life and death. Aaron ran into the middle of a dying crowd with his censer, making atonement, stopping the plague. That's what prayer does. That's what Jesus does for us: standing between judgment and mercy, interceding so we might live. And we're called to do the same for others.

Fifth, God provides cleansing for inevitable contamination. Living in this world means encountering death, both physical and spiritual. We can't avoid it. But God doesn't leave us stuck in our uncleanness. He provides ways to be made clean again. In Christ, no matter how contaminated we feel, no matter how many times we've failed, there is cleansing available. The red heifer ashes could be used over and over; the cleansing Christ provides is inexhaustible. As 1 John promises: "If we confess our sins, he is faithful and just and will forgive us our sins and purify us from all unrighteousness" (1 John 1:9). That verse ends with a period, not a comma. No exceptions. Full and final cleansing is available in Jesus.

TALKING POINTS

1. **God gave the Israelites tassels to wear as visual reminders of his commands.** What "reminders" do you have in your life that help you remember who you belong to and how you're called to live?

2. **Korah argued that "the whole community is holy" and questioned why Moses and Aaron should have special authority.** Why was this argument wrong, even though it sounded fair? What's the difference between everyone being valuable to God and everyone having the same role?

3. **Aaron ran into the middle of a plague to make atonement for the very people who had been grumbling against him.** What does this teach us about how to respond to people who have wronged us?

4. **The red heifer ritual provided cleansing that was freely available to the whole community.** How does this picture of "free cleansing" point forward to what Jesus provides?

5. **After watching the ground swallow the rebels and fire consume their supporters, the people complained that Moses had "killed the LORD's people."** Why is it so hard for humans to accept God's judgment, even when it's clearly from him?

The rebellion had been crushed. The priesthood had been confirmed. Provisions for cleansing had been made. But the forty years of wandering were just beginning. What would happen when the people faced new challenges? Would they trust God this time? Would Moses himself remain faithful under pressure?

The next chapter reveals a painful answer. Turn the page.

7

THE BRONZE SERPENT

Near the end of *Avengers: Endgame*, Tony Stark has a choice. He can snap his fingers with the Infinity Gauntlet and save the universe—but it will kill him. He's fought countless battles. He's sacrificed everything. And in his final moment, he does what needs to be done to save everyone else.

But what if, after all that heroism, Tony had made a terrible choice? What if, in a moment of frustration or pride, he'd done something that disqualified him from being there at the end?

That's essentially what happens to Moses in Numbers 20. Moses is the greatest hero in Israel's story so far. He faced down Pharaoh. He led the people through the Red Sea. He climbed Mount Sinai and received God's law. He interceded again and again for rebellious people who didn't deserve his prayers. For forty years, he faithfully guided millions of complainers through the wilderness. And then, just before the finish line, he stumbled. And it cost him everything.

Numbers 20–21 is one of the most dramatic sections in the entire Bible. It contains the death of Miriam, Moses' devastating failure, the death of Aaron, poisonous snakes, a bronze serpent, and military victories that finally—*finally*—move Israel toward the Promised Land.

These chapters mark the transition from one generation to the next. The old guard is passing away. New leaders are rising. And through it all, we see both the consequences of faithlessness and the surprising ways God provides healing and hope.

MIRIAM'S DEATH AND THE COMPLAINT AT MERIBAH

The chapter opens with a death notice, almost casual in its brevity: "There Miriam died and was buried." Miriam, Moses' sister, the one who watched over him as a baby floating in the Nile, the one who led the women in celebration after crossing the Red Sea. She was one of the three primary leaders of Israel (along with Moses and Aaron). And now, in a single sentence, she's gone.

The forty years of wandering are nearly over. The first generation is dying off, just as God said they would. Miriam's death signals that the transition has begun.

Almost immediately, the old pattern resurfaces: the people had no water, and they gathered against Moses and Aaron. "If only we had died when our brothers fell dead before the LORD!"

Think about what they're saying. They wished they had died in the recent rebellions—the ones where the ground swallowed people and fire consumed others. They were saying, "Being destroyed by God's judgment would have been better than being here with you."

Their complaints piled up: "Why did you bring us out of Egypt? Why did you bring us to this terrible place? There's no grain, no figs, no pomegranates, and no water!"

Notice the irony. They were complaining that the wilderness didn't have figs and pomegranates—the very fruits the spies had brought back from Canaan forty years earlier. They could have been in the land that had those things. They refused to go. Now they blamed Moses for the consequences of their own choice.

Moses and Aaron did what they'd done before: they went to the tent of meeting and fell facedown before God. The glory of the LORD appeared, and God gave Moses instructions. "Take the staff. Gather the assembly. Speak to that rock before their eyes and it will pour out its water."

Simple enough. Take the staff—probably Aaron's budding staff that was kept in the tabernacle as a sign of God's power. Gather the people. Speak to the rock. Water would flow.

But that's not what Moses did.

MOSES' COSTLY MISTAKE

Moses gathered the people. He stood before the rock with Aaron beside him. And then something went wrong. "Listen, you rebels," Moses shouted at the crowd. "Must *we* bring you water out of this rock?" Then he raised his arm and struck the rock. Twice. Water gushed out. The people and their livestock drank. Crisis solved.

But God's response was devastating: "Because you did not trust in me enough to honor me as holy in the sight of the Israelites, you will not bring this community into the land I give them."

Moses—the faithful servant, the intercessor, the leader who had given forty years of his life to this ungrateful nation—would not enter the Promised Land. Neither would Aaron.

What went so wrong?

Several things, actually. First, God had said to speak to the rock. Moses struck it twice. That might seem like a minor difference, but obedience isn't about getting close to what God said. It's about doing what God said.

Second, look at what Moses said: "Must *we* bring you water?" Not "God will provide." Not "Watch what the LORD does." Moses made it sound like he and Aaron were the ones with the power. After decades of pointing people to God, in this moment Moses pointed people to himself.

Third, the text says Moses "raised his arm"—the same language used elsewhere to describe defiant sin. This wasn't a slip of the tongue. Moses was angry, and his anger led him to take matters into his own hands.

In his frustration with the people (and honestly, who could blame him for being frustrated?), Moses drew attention to himself instead of pointing to God. He took credit that belonged to God. He failed to treat God as holy—as utterly distinct, utterly unique, the only one with the power to save.

After forty years of faithful service, in one moment of frustration, Moses sinned publicly before the entire nation. And because leaders are held to a higher standard, because what leaders do shapes how people think about God, the consequences were severe.

The place was named Meribah, meaning "quarreling." God still provided water. God is gracious even when his servants fail. But Moses would see the Promised Land only from a distance. He would never set foot in it.

EDOM'S REFUSAL AND AARON'S DEATH

The journey continued. Moses sent messengers to Edom, asking permission to pass through their territory. Edom was descended from Esau, Jacob's brother, making them Israel's relatives. Moses' appeal was respectful: "You know about all the hardships we've faced. Please let us pass through. We won't touch your fields or wells. We'll stay on the main road."

Edom's answer was flat: "No. And if you try, we'll attack you."

Israel asked again, even offering to pay for any water they used. Edom refused again and marched out with a large army to enforce the refusal.

Israel turned away. They could have fought—God had promised them victory over enemies—but Edom wasn't the enemy. They were family, however hostile. So Israel took the long way around.

Then came another death. At Mount Hor, God told Moses that Aaron would die. Just as Miriam's death had opened the chapter, Aaron's death would close it. Both of Moses' siblings were gone.

The transfer of leadership was public and deliberate. Moses took Aaron and his son Eleazar up the mountain while the whole community watched. Moses removed Aaron's priestly garments and put them on Eleazar. Then Aaron died.

Moses and Eleazar came down the mountain alone. The people mourned for thirty days.

The old generation was passing. The high priesthood continued, but with new hands. And Moses himself was now under a death sentence, not by plague or fire, but by God's decree. He would not set foot in the Promised Land.

VICTORY AT HORMAH AND THE BRONZE SERPENT

Chapter 21 opens with a small victory. The Canaanite king of Arad attacked Israel and captured some prisoners. This time, instead of panicking or complaining, Israel prayed. "If you will deliver these people into our hands, we will totally destroy their cities."

God answered. Israel won. They named the place Hormah, "destruction." It was a sign of what was possible when Israel trusted God instead of fearing enemies.

But the grumbling wasn't over.

As they traveled south to go around Edom, the people grew impatient. The route was long. The terrain was harsh. And once again, the complaints came out: "Why have you brought us up out of Egypt to die in the wilderness? There is no bread! There is no water! And we detest this miserable food!"

The "miserable food" was manna, the same miraculous bread from heaven that had sustained them for forty years. They hated it. They were sick of God's provision.

This time, God's response was immediate and terrifying: venomous snakes. The snakes spread through the camp, biting people. Many died. The Hebrew describes them as "fiery" snakes, possibly referring to the burning sensation of their venom or to their quick, striking movement.

The people rushed to Moses: "We sinned! We spoke against the LORD and against you. Pray that the LORD will take the snakes away!"

Moses prayed. But God's solution wasn't what anyone expected. "Make a snake and put it up on a pole. Anyone who is bitten can look at it and live." Moses made a bronze serpent and mounted it on a pole. From then on, when someone was bitten, they could look at the bronze snake and survive.

This sounds strange to modern readers. Why make an image of the very thing killing them? But the point wasn't the bronze itself, it was the looking. It was faith expressed through a specific action. The snake on the pole was God's appointed means of healing. Those who looked, lived. Those who refused—whether from pride or stubbornness or disbelief—died.

The bronze serpent couldn't save anyone by its own power. It was just metal. But God had declared it to be the means of salvation, and looking at it in faith was how you received what God offered. You couldn't earn healing by being good enough. You couldn't buy it. You simply had to look at what God provided and trust him.

Centuries later, Jesus pointed to this event to explain his own mission: "Just as Moses lifted up the snake in the wilderness, so the Son of Man must be lifted up, that everyone who believes may have eternal life" (John 3:14–15). The bronze serpent was a picture. Jesus on the cross is the reality. We've all been bitten by sin, its poison is working in us, leading to death. The cure isn't self-improvement or good behavior. The cure is looking in faith at the one who was lifted up for us. Look and live.

VICTORIES OVER SIHON AND OG

The remainder of chapter 21 describes Israel's journey northward and two major military victories.

First, they encountered Sihon, king of the Amorites. Like with Edom, Israel asked for peaceful passage. Unlike Edom, Sihon attacked. This time Israel fought back and won decisively. They captured Sihon's territory, including his capital city of Heshbon.

Then came Og, king of Bashan, ruling territory northeast of the Sea of Galilee. God gave clear instructions: "Do not fear him, for I have delivered him into your hands." Israel obeyed. They defeated Og and took his land.

These victories were significant. For the first time, Israel was conquering territory. They were acting like the nation God had called them to be: trusting his promises, fighting his battles, taking land he was giving them. Later psalms would celebrate these victories as proof of God's faithfulness.

The chapter ends with Israel camped on the plains of Moab, just across the Jordan River from Jericho. After forty years of wandering, they were finally within sight of the Promised Land.

WHAT THIS MEANS FOR US

First, even the greatest servants can fail at the finish line. Moses' failure is sobering. Decades of faithfulness didn't make him immune to sin. One moment of frustration, one act of pride, and he forfeited the prize he'd worked toward his whole life. This isn't meant to discourage us; it's meant to keep us humble. No one is beyond falling. Guard your heart, especially when you're tired and frustrated.

Second, leaders are held to a higher standard. This might seem unfair, but it makes sense. What leaders do shapes how people think about God. When Moses made it look like he was the source of water instead of God, he misrepresented God to the entire nation. When you're in any position of leadership, take that responsibility seriously. People are watching, and what they see shapes what they believe.

Third, the consequences of our choices can last even after forgiveness. Moses was still God's servant. God still spoke with him. The relationship wasn't destroyed. But the consequence stood: Moses wouldn't enter the land. Forgiveness is real. Grace is abundant. But that doesn't mean we escape all consequences of our actions.

Fourth, looking in faith is the way to life. The bronze serpent couldn't heal anyone by itself. It was just metal on a pole. But looking at it in obedience to God's command brought healing. Faith isn't magic. Faith is trusting God's appointed means of salvation. For Israel, it was a bronze snake. For us, it's the cross. Jesus said it directly: look at him, trust in him, obey him, and live.

Fifth, victory comes when we trust God's promises. Israel's military victories in chapter 21 happened because they believed God when he said, "Do not fear. I have delivered them into your hands." When we face overwhelming opposition, the question isn't whether we're strong enough. The question is whether we'll trust the God who fights for us.

TALKING POINTS

1. **Moses struck the rock instead of speaking to it and said "must we bring you water?"** Why do you think this was such a serious offense? What does it teach us about taking credit that belongs to God?

2. **Even after forty years of faithful leadership, Moses disqualified himself from entering the Promised Land through**

one act of disobedience. What does this tell us about the danger of letting frustration and anger control our actions?

3. **When the Israelites were bitten by snakes, God's solution wasn't to remove the snakes but to provide a way of healing through looking at the bronze serpent.** Why do you think God sometimes allows difficult circumstances to continue while providing a way through them rather than removing them entirely?

4. **Jesus compared himself to the bronze serpent: "Just as Moses lifted up the snake in the wilderness, so the Son of Man must be lifted up."** What does this comparison teach us about how salvation works?

5. **Israel defeated Sihon and Og after trusting God's promise that he had delivered the enemies into their hands.** How can remembering past victories help us face current challenges with faith instead of fear?

Israel was camped on the edge of the Promised Land. They had won battles. They had conquered territory. The old generation was nearly gone, and the new generation was ready to move forward.

But before they could cross the Jordan, they would face an enemy they couldn't fight with swords: a prophet hired to curse them. What Balaam expected to happen, and what actually happened, would become one of the strangest and most memorable stories in the entire Bible.

Turn the page.

8

THE PROPHET AND THE TALKING DONKEY

In *Shrek*, there's a talking donkey named Donkey who sees things his companions miss. He's annoying, sure, but he's also often right. When Shrek can't see what's obvious, Donkey points it out. When danger is coming, Donkey notices first.

Numbers 22–24 has a talking donkey too. But this one isn't comic relief. This donkey sees an angel with a drawn sword that her master, a famous prophet, is completely blind to. And when God opens her mouth to speak, she wins an argument with a professional seer.

It's one of the strangest stories in the entire Bible. And also one of the funniest. But behind the humor is something deadly serious. A pagan king has hired the ancient world's most famous curse-for-hire prophet to destroy Israel with words. What happens next reveals something important: when God decides to bless someone, no one—no matter how powerful or famous—can reverse it.

This is the story of Balaam and Balak. It involves a terrified king, a greedy prophet, a donkey smarter than her owner, and four prophecies that backfire spectacularly on the person who paid for them.

BALAK'S PLAN TO CURSE ISRAEL

The Moabites were terrified. They had watched Israel defeat the Amorites. They had seen what happened to King Sihon and King Og. Now this massive army was camped right on their border, and they knew they couldn't win a straight fight.

King Balak of Moab needed a different strategy. If he couldn't defeat Israel with swords, maybe he could defeat them with words. Specifically, with a curse.

In the ancient world, people believed that blessings and curses had real power. A curse spoken by the right person, with the right rituals, could bring disaster on an enemy. And there was one man famous throughout the region for his effective curses: a prophet named Balaam, who lived about 400 miles away near the Euphrates River.

Balak sent messengers with a fee for divination—payment for Balaam's services. The message was simple: "A people has come out of Egypt. They cover the face of the land. Come, put a curse on them for me. Maybe then I can defeat them. I know that whoever you bless is blessed, and whoever you curse is cursed." Balaam told the messengers to spend the night. He would see what "the LORD" had to say.

That night, God spoke to Balaam directly: "Do not go with them. You must not put a curse on those people, because they are blessed." Balaam sent the messengers away.

But Balak wasn't done. He sent more messengers (more distinguished ones) with promises of greater rewards. "I will reward you handsomely," the message said. "Do whatever you say. Just come and curse these people."

Balaam's response sounded pious: "Even if Balak gave me

all the silver and gold in his palace, I could not do anything to go beyond the command of the LORD my God." But notice what he did next: instead of simply saying no, he told them to stay the night again so he could see if God might change his mind. That's a red flag. When God says no, why ask again—unless you're hoping for a different answer?

This time, God told him to go. But he added a warning: "Do only what I tell you." Balaam saddled his donkey and headed out. He was going to get paid after all.

THE DONKEY WHO SAW WHAT THE PROPHET COULDN'T

But God was angry. The text says God's anger burned because Balaam went. That seems confusing—didn't God just give him permission? But the clue is in what happens next. God knew Balaam's heart. Balaam wasn't going to faithfully deliver God's message. He was going to try to earn his fee by cursing Israel if he possibly could.

So God sent an angel to block the road. The angel stood in the path with a drawn sword. The donkey saw him. Balaam didn't. The donkey turned off the road into a field. Balaam beat her to get her back on track.

The angel moved to a narrow path between two vineyard walls. The donkey pressed against the wall, crushing Balaam's foot. He beat her again. The angel moved to a place so narrow there was no room to go around. The donkey just lay down. Balaam lost his temper and beat her with his staff.

Then God opened the donkey's mouth. "What have I done to you to make you beat me three times?"

Stop and appreciate how absurd this is. A famous prophet

is having a conversation with his donkey. And he's so angry he doesn't even seem surprised that she's talking. "You have made a fool of me!" Balaam shouted. "If I had a sword, I would kill you right now!"

The irony is thick. Balaam said he wished he had a sword—while an angel with an actual sword was standing right there, ready to kill *him*. The donkey had saved his life three times, and he wanted to kill her for it.

The donkey made a logical argument: "Am I not your own donkey, which you have always ridden? Have I been in the habit of doing this to you?" Balaam had to admit: "No." Then God opened Balaam's eyes. He saw the angel with the drawn sword and fell facedown.

The angel explained: "I have come to oppose you because your path is reckless before me. The donkey saw me and turned away three times. If she hadn't, I would have killed you by now, but I would have spared her." Think about that. The donkey was innocent. The prophet was guilty. The animal was more spiritually perceptive than the professional seer.

Balaam said, "I have sinned. I'll go back if you want." The angel told him to continue, but with a warning: "Speak only what I tell you." The message was clear: obey exactly, or die.

THE FIRST ORACLE

Balaam arrived in Moab, and Balak was annoyed. "Didn't I send you an urgent summons? Why didn't you come immediately?" Balaam's answer was crucial: "I can't say whatever I please. I must speak only what God puts in my mouth."

Balak didn't care. He wanted his curse. He took Balaam to

a high place where they could look down on the Israelite camp. Balaam told him to build seven altars and sacrifice seven bulls and seven rams—the full ritual treatment. Then Balaam went off alone to meet with God.

God met with him. And he gave Balaam a message. Balaam returned and delivered his first oracle, but it wasn't a curse. It was a blessing. "How can I curse those whom God has not cursed? How can I denounce those whom the LORD has not denounced? I see a people who live apart and do not consider themselves one of the nations. Who can count the dust of Jacob? Let me die the death of the righteous, and may my final end be like theirs!"

Balak was furious. "What have you done to me? I brought you to curse my enemies, but you have done nothing but bless them!" Balaam shrugged: "Must I not speak what the LORD puts in my mouth?"

THE SECOND ORACLE

Balak tried again. Maybe a different location would produce different results. He took Balaam to another high place, built seven more altars, offered seven more bulls and seven more rams. Balaam went to meet with God. God gave him another message.

The second oracle was even stronger: "God is not human, that he should lie, not a human being, that he should change his mind. Does he speak and then not act? Does he promise and not fulfill? I have received a command to bless; he has blessed, and I cannot change it. No misfortune is seen in Jacob, no misery observed in Israel. The LORD their God is with them; the shout of the King is among them."

Balaam was saying: I can't curse them because God has already blessed them. And God doesn't change his mind. You're fighting against the God of the universe, Balak. You can't win this.

He continued: "God brought them out of Egypt; they have the strength of a wild ox. There is no divination against Jacob, no evil omens against Israel." That last line was devastating for Balak. He had hired Balaam specifically for his skill with omens and divination. And now Balaam was telling him that such methods simply don't work against Israel. Their God is too powerful. No curse, no spell, no ritual can overcome what God has decided to do.

Balak's response was almost desperate: "Neither curse them at all nor bless them at all!" In other words: if you can't curse them, at least stop blessing them! But Balaam couldn't stop. God had given him words, and he had to speak them.

THE THIRD AND FOURTH ORACLES

Balak tried one more time. New location. Seven more altars. Seven more bulls and rams. Same result. But this time, something changed in Balaam. He didn't go off looking for omens. He turned and faced the Israelite camp, and the Spirit of God came on him. His eyes were opened in a way they hadn't been before, and he spoke his most beautiful oracle yet:

"How beautiful are your tents, Jacob, your dwelling places, Israel! Like valleys they spread out, like gardens beside a river, like aloes planted by the LORD, like cedars beside the waters. Water will flow from their buckets; their seed will have abundant water. Their king will be greater than Agag; their kingdom will be exalted."

He finished by echoing the ancient promise God made to Abraham: "May those who bless you be blessed and those who curse you be cursed!"

Balak exploded. He struck his hands together in rage. "I summoned you to curse my enemies, but you have blessed them three times! Now leave! I said I would reward you handsomely, but the LORD has kept you from being rewarded."

Balaam wasn't finished. Before leaving, he delivered one final oracle—a prophecy about the future: "I see him, but not now; I behold him, but not near. A star will come out of Jacob; a scepter will rise out of Israel."

This prophecy pointed to a coming king who would defeat all of Israel's enemies. It found initial fulfillment in King David centuries later, but its ultimate fulfillment would be in someone far greater. When the wise men came looking for the newborn "king of the Jews" in Matthew 2, following a star, they were unknowingly connecting to this ancient prophecy spoken by a pagan prophet who couldn't curse God's people no matter how hard he tried.

The irony is extraordinary. Balak hired Balaam to destroy Israel's future. Instead, Balaam prophesied about Israel's greatest king, and ultimately about the Messiah who would save not just Israel but the whole world.

Balaam's final oracle predicted doom for Moab, Edom, Amalek, and other nations who opposed Israel. The very people who tried to curse Israel would themselves experience destruction. Then Balaam went home, and Balak went away—without his curse, watching his enemy blessed more powerfully than ever.

WHAT THIS MEANS FOR US

First, when God blesses someone, no one can reverse it. Balak thought spiritual power could be bought and manipulated. He thought the right prophet with the right rituals could override God's will. He was completely wrong. God's blessing on his people is secure. As Paul would later write: "If God is for us, who can be against us?" (Romans 8:31).

Second, correct words don't guarantee a right heart. Balaam said all the right things. He claimed he could only speak what God commanded. He delivered accurate prophecies. He even expressed a desire to "die the death of the righteous." But his heart was greedy, and later he would find another way to harm Israel—by advising Moab to seduce them into idolatry and immorality (Numbers 31:16). Speaking truth doesn't mean you love truth. Even Satan can quote Scripture. What matters is whether your heart belongs to God. Jesus warned about people who prophesy in his name and perform miracles, yet he tells them, "I never knew you" (Matthew 7:22–23). Knowing about God isn't the same as knowing God.

Third, God can speak through anyone—or anything. If God can speak through a donkey, he can use anyone to accomplish his purposes. This doesn't mean we should listen to donkeys for spiritual advice. But it does mean we shouldn't be surprised when God uses unexpected people or circumstances to get our attention.

Fourth, trying to manipulate God is foolish. Balak kept trying different locations and more sacrifices, hoping to get different results. But God isn't a vending machine where the right combination of inputs produces the desired output. He's the sovereign Lord of the universe. You don't manipulate him; you submit to him.

Fifth, God's purposes will be accomplished despite human opposition. Balak did everything he could to curse Israel. He hired the best prophet money could buy. He built altars and offered sacrifices. He tried three different locations. And every single attempt backfired. When God decides to bless, all the opposition in the world can't stop it.

TALKING POINTS

1. **Balaam's donkey could see the angel when Balaam couldn't.** What do you think this says about spiritual perception? Is it possible for "ordinary" people to sometimes see spiritual realities that "experts" miss?

2. **Balaam said all the right words about only speaking what God commanded, but his heart was motivated by greed.** How can we tell the difference between genuine faith and religious performance? What are some warning signs that someone's words don't match their heart?

3. **Balak kept trying different locations and more sacrifices, hoping to get a different result from God.** Why do people sometimes think they can manipulate God through rituals or religious activities? What's wrong with that approach?

4. **The prophecy about a "star" and "scepter" from Jacob ultimately points to Jesus.** What does it mean that this prophecy came through a pagan prophet who was trying to curse Israel? What does this tell us about God's ability to accomplish his purposes?

5. **God's blessing on Israel couldn't be reversed by the most famous curse-prophet in the ancient world.** How should this affect the way we think about opposition we face as God's people today?

Israel had been blessed—powerfully, publicly, irrevocably. An enemy king's worst weapon had backfired completely. But the battle wasn't over. Balaam may have failed to curse Israel with words, but he would find another way to harm them. The next chapter reveals how, and the consequences would be devastating.

Turn the page.

9

SEDUCTION, CENSUS, AND SUCCESSION

In *The Lord of the Rings*, after Gandalf falls fighting the Balrog, the Fellowship faces a devastating question: Who will lead them now? Aragorn steps up, but he's not Gandalf. The loss reshapes everything. The group must move forward, but nothing feels the same.

Numbers 25–27 deals with similar transitions, but darker ones. The generation that left Egypt is finally, truly passing away. Moses himself will not cross into the Promised Land. New leaders must rise. A new census must count who's left. And the people must prepare for a future without the man who has led them for forty years.

But before any of that can happen, there's one final disaster. Balaam may have failed to curse Israel, but he found another way to hurt them, and it nearly destroyed everything.

THE SEDUCTION AT BAAL-PEOR

Remember Balaam? The prophet hired to curse Israel who kept blessing them instead? He went home without his payment. But the story doesn't end there.

Later we learn that Balaam gave Moab some advice: if you can't curse Israel, seduce them. Get them to sin against their own God. Then God himself will punish them, and you won't need a curse at all.

It worked.

While Israel was camped at Shittim, on the edge of the Promised Land, Moabite and Midianite women began inviting Israelite men to worship with them. The "worship" involved sexual immorality and then participation in sacrifices to Baal, the Canaanite fertility god. The women drew the men in with sex, and the sex led to idolatry.

The text says Israel "yoked themselves to the Baal of Peor." Picture two oxen yoked together, pulling in the same direction. Israel was supposed to be yoked to the Lord, bound exclusively to him in covenant love. Instead, they hitched themselves to a foreign god. It was spiritual adultery, and God's anger burned against them.

A plague broke out. The Lord told Moses to execute the leaders who had led the people into this sin and expose their bodies publicly, a sign that they were under God's curse. The judgment was severe because the sin was severe.

Then something happened that made everything worse. While Moses and the people were weeping at the entrance of the tent of meeting—mourning the plague, seeking God's forgiveness—an Israelite man walked right past them with a Midianite woman on his arm. In full view of everyone, he took her into his tent. This wasn't ignorance. This was defiance. The whole community was repenting, and this man was publicly continuing the very sin that had brought the plague.

Phinehas, the grandson of Aaron the high priest, saw it. He grabbed a spear, followed the couple into the tent, and drove the spear through both of them. The plague stopped. But 24,000 people had already died.

PHINEHAS' ZEAL AND GOD'S COVENANT

God's response to Phinehas might surprise us. He commended him. "Phinehas has turned my anger away from the Israelites. He was as zealous for my honor among them as I am."

The word "zealous" here is related to the word "jealous." This isn't petty jealousy; it's the righteous anger of a husband whose wife has been publicly unfaithful. God had entered into a covenant with Israel, like a marriage. They had promised exclusive loyalty. And they had just committed adultery with other gods, in public, while people were dying because of that very sin.

Phinehas shared God's righteous anger. He acted to stop the sin and the judgment it brought. As a result, God gave him and his descendants a "covenant of peace"—a guarantee that his family line would continue serving as priests.

The severity of God's response might trouble us. Why 24,000 dead? Why such extreme measures? The answer lies in understanding what was at stake. Israel wasn't just a nation—they were God's chosen instrument to bless the whole world. Through them, all nations would eventually be blessed. When they abandoned God for idols, they were sabotaging their mission. They were closing off the channel through which God's blessing would flow to everyone else. God's severe discipline of Israel was, in a strange way, an expression of his love for the entire world. He was pruning his vine so it would bear fruit for everyone.

The chapter ends by naming the guilty parties: Zimri, the Israelite man, was a leader in the tribe of Simeon. Kozbi, the Midianite woman, was the daughter of a tribal chief. These weren't nobodies sneaking around. They were prominent people, flaunting their sin in front of everyone. Their public defiance required public justice.

God then declared that Midian should be treated as an enemy because they had treated Israel as an enemy, using seduction as a weapon to destroy God's people from within.

THE SECOND CENSUS: A GENERATION PASSES

Chapter 26 records a second census. Nearly forty years had passed since the first census in Numbers 1. That census counted the generation that left Egypt, the generation that refused to enter the Promised Land and was condemned to die in the wilderness. Now, with that judgment complete, it was time to count who remained.

The results tell a story. The total number was almost exactly the same as before: 601,730 compared to 603,550. Israel had neither grown nor shrunk significantly. But within that total, individual tribes had changed dramatically. Simeon, whose leader Zimri had just been executed, had lost 63% of its population—dropping from 59,300 to 22,200. Manasseh had grown 64%. Some tribes gained; others declined.

The chapter notes several times that certain family lines ended in judgment: Dathan and Abiram, who rebelled with Korah and were swallowed by the earth. Er and Onan, who died in Canaan for their sins. Nadab and Abihu, Aaron's sons, who offered unauthorized fire and were consumed. These weren't random deaths. They were warnings built into the genealogy itself.

But there's also grace woven through the census. "The line of Korah, however, did not die out." Even though Korah himself was judged, his descendants continued. Centuries later, some of his descendants would write psalms that are still in our Bibles today.

The most important statement comes at the end: "Not one of them was among those counted by Moses and Aaron the priest when they counted the Israelites in the Desert of Sinai… except Caleb son of Jephunneh and Joshua son of Nun."

The old generation was gone. Every single person from that first census had died in the wilderness—except two. The two scouts who trusted God when everyone else gave in to fear. The two who said, "We can certainly take the land." They alone survived to see the promise fulfilled.

The census wasn't just about numbers. It was proof that God keeps his word, both in judgment and in blessing.

It also served a practical purpose: the land would be divided according to the census numbers. Larger tribes would receive larger portions. Smaller tribes would receive smaller portions. And the actual distribution would be done by lot, essentially letting God decide which specific territory each tribe would receive. No one could complain that they got a bad deal, because God himself had assigned each inheritance.

This is the pattern throughout Scripture: God gives his people an inheritance as a gift. They don't earn it. They receive it with gratitude. Comparing your inheritance to someone else's misses the point entirely—it was a gift from God, and gifts are meant to be received with thankfulness, not measured against what others received.

ZELOPHEHAD'S DAUGHTERS: A CASE FOR JUSTICE

Chapter 27 opens with a problem: five sisters with no brothers and a dead father. Zelophehad had died in the wilderness—not for rebellion like Korah's followers, but as part of the general judgment on that generation. He left behind five daughters: Mahlah, Noah, Hoglah, Milkah, and Tirzah. No sons.

In that culture, land passed from father to son. Without a son, Zelophehad's family would lose their share of the Promised Land entirely. His name would disappear from his clan.

The daughters went to Moses with a bold request: "Why should our father's name disappear from his clan because he had no son? Give us property among our father's relatives."

This took courage. They were challenging an established cultural practice. They were standing before Moses, Eleazar the priest, and all the leaders—five women asking for something women didn't normally receive. They believed God's promise about the land strongly enough to fight for their family's share of it.

Moses took their case to the Lord. And God's answer was clear: "What Zelophehad's daughters are saying is right. You must certainly give them property as an inheritance among their father's relatives." God then expanded this into a general law: if a man dies without sons, his inheritance goes to his daughters. If no daughters, then to his brothers. If no brothers, to his father's brothers. If none of them, to the nearest relative. The land must stay in the family. No one's inheritance should simply disappear.

This ruling was remarkable for its time. It showed that God's concern was for justice and for people, not rigid adherence to cultural patterns. When existing rules caused injustice, God made new rules.

JOSHUA COMMISSIONED

Then came the hardest transition of all. "Go up into the Abarim mountains," God told Moses, "and see the land I have given the Israelites. After you have seen it, you too will be gathered to your people, as your brother Aaron was."

Moses would see the Promised Land, but only from a distance. He would not enter it. The sin at Meribah, where he struck the rock instead of speaking to it, had cost him that privilege.

How did Moses respond? Not with argument or complaint. He prayed for the people. "May the LORD, the God who gives breath to all living things, appoint someone over this community to go out and come in before them, one who will lead them out and bring them in, so the LORD's people will not be like sheep without a shepherd."

Even facing his own death, Moses' concern was for Israel. They needed a leader. Without one, they would be scattered and destroyed, sheep without a shepherd.

God's answer: Joshua. Joshua had been Moses' assistant since his youth. He had fought battles, scouted the land, and stood firm when everyone else panicked. God said he was "a man in whom is the spirit," already equipped for leadership.

The commissioning was public. Moses laid his hands on Joshua before Eleazar the priest and the whole assembly. He transferred some of his authority to Joshua so the people would know to follow him. The succession was official.

But there was a difference. Moses had spoken with God face to face—directly, clearly, without riddles. Joshua would need to inquire through the priest, using the Urim and Thummim—sacred lots kept in the high priest's breastplate—to discern God's direction. Joshua was a great leader, but he wasn't Moses. No one was. There would never be another prophet quite like Moses until centuries later, when another prophet came who spoke with God face to face: Jesus himself.

Moses did exactly as God commanded. Joshua was commissioned. The people had their next leader. And in this moment of transition, we see something beautiful: Moses didn't resent being replaced. He didn't cling to power. He prayed for his successor's appointment and then publicly supported him. That's the heart of a true shepherd: someone who cares more about the flock than about his own position.

WHAT THIS MEANS FOR US

First, seduction is often more dangerous than frontal assault. Balaam couldn't curse Israel, so he advised seduction instead. The enemy often works the same way today—not through obvious attacks but through gradual enticement. The path to serious sin usually starts with small compromises that seem harmless.

Second, sin is personal betrayal, not just rule-breaking. The language the Bible uses for idolatry is the language of adultery. When we put anything ahead of God—whether literal idols or modern substitutes like money, status, or pleasure—

we're not just breaking a rule. We're betraying a relationship. We're being unfaithful to someone who loves us.

Third, God's judgment and blessing both prove his faithfulness. The first generation died in the wilderness because God said they would. Caleb and Joshua survived because God said they would. God keeps his word—always. That's terrifying if you're on the wrong side of it. It's deeply comforting if you're trusting his promises.

Fourth, God cares about justice for the marginalized. Zelophehad's daughters were in a vulnerable position: women without male relatives to protect their inheritance. They could have been overlooked. Instead, God ruled in their favor and changed the law to protect others in similar situations. He sees those the system overlooks.

Fifth, good leaders prepare for succession. Moses' final act of leadership was ensuring the people had a leader after him. He didn't cling to power or leave the transition to chance. He prayed, he commissioned Joshua publicly, and he made the handoff clear. The mark of a great leader isn't just what they accomplish; it's what continues after they're gone.

TALKING POINTS

1. **Balaam couldn't curse Israel, so he advised using seduction instead.** Why do you think temptation that comes gradually is often more dangerous than obvious attacks? How can we guard against slow compromises?

2. **Phinehas acted with violent zeal to stop sin and the plague it brought.** How do we understand his actions? What's the difference between righteous anger and sinful anger?

3. **Zelophehad's daughters challenged cultural practice and asked for their inheritance.** What does it take to advocate for justice when existing systems don't serve everyone fairly? What gave these women the courage to speak up?

4. **Moses was told he would die without entering the Promised Land, and his response was to pray for his successor.** What does this reveal about his character? How would you have responded in his situation?

5. **The census showed that the entire first generation had died except Caleb and Joshua.** What does it mean to live as someone who trusts God's promises even when everyone around you doesn't?

The transitions were complete. The sinners had been judged. The people had been counted. The daughters had received justice. Joshua had been commissioned.

Israel was ready to move forward. But first, God had more instructions for them about worship, vows, and the inheritance of the tribes east of the Jordan. The preparations for entering the land were almost finished.

Turn the page.

10

READY FOR THE PROMISED LAND

At the end of every school year, there's a moment when teachers stop introducing new material and start reviewing. They go over everything you've learned. They prepare you for final exams. They make sure you're ready for the next grade.

That's essentially what happens in Numbers 28–36. The wilderness journey is almost over. Israel is camped on the plains of Moab, looking across the Jordan River at the Promised Land. Before they cross, God gives them final instructions: reviewing old laws, adding new ones, and preparing them for life in their new home.

These chapters might seem like a grab bag of random topics: festival calendars, rules about vows, a war with Midian, tribal territories, cities of refuge, and a final ruling about daughters inheriting land. But there's a theme connecting all of it: preparing God's people to live with him in the land he promised them.

The wilderness was never meant to be permanent. It was always headed somewhere. And now that "somewhere" is finally in sight.

THE CALENDAR OF WORSHIP

Numbers 28–29 gives Israel a detailed calendar of worship. Think about it: they're about to enter a new land where they'll plant crops, build houses, and settle down. They won't be following the cloud anymore. How will they stay connected to God in this new life?

The answer is rhythm. Daily, weekly, monthly, and yearly patterns of worship that structure their entire lives around God.

Every single day, priests would offer a lamb in the morning and another at twilight, along with grain and wine offerings. These daily sacrifices weren't optional. They were the heartbeat of Israel's relationship with God. Morning and evening, every day, the smoke rising from the altar reminded everyone that they belonged to a God who wanted to dwell among them.

Every week, the Sabbath brought additional offerings and a day of complete rest. Unlike the nations around them, Israel marked time by a seven-day week ending in worship and rest, a pattern established at creation itself.

Every month, the new moon was marked with special sacrifices. And throughout the year, major festivals punctuated the calendar:

Passover and Unleavened Bread (spring): remembering the exodus from Egypt

Feast of Weeks (early summer): celebrating the wheat harvest

Feast of Trumpets (fall): beginning the most sacred month with trumpet blasts

Day of Atonement (fall): the one day each year when the high priest entered the Most Holy Place to make atonement for all Israel's sins

Feast of Tabernacles (fall): a week-long celebration of the harvest, where people lived in temporary shelters to remember the wilderness journey

The Feast of Tabernacles was the biggest celebration of the year. Over the eight days, they sacrificed a total of 71 bulls, 15 rams, 105 lambs, and 8 goats—more animals than any other festival. The sheer abundance expressed joy and thanksgiving for God's provision.

All these rhythms served the same purpose: to keep God at the center of life. In the busyness of farming and building and raising families, the calendar of worship would regularly interrupt normal activities and redirect attention to God. They would never be allowed to forget who had brought them to this land and who sustained them in it.

THE SERIOUSNESS OF VOWS

Chapter 30 addresses vows—promises made to God. Vows were serious business. When you made a promise to God, you were expected to keep it. The chapter says plainly: "When a man makes a vow to the LORD or takes an oath to obligate himself by a pledge, he must not break his word but must do everything he said."

But what about women and girls? In that culture, women lived under the authority of their fathers (if unmarried) or husbands (if married). The chapter explains that a father could nullify his daughter's vow if he heard it and objected immediately. A husband could do the same for his wife. But if the man heard the vow and said nothing, it stood. His silence counted as approval, and the woman was bound to fulfill it.

This might seem unfair to modern readers. Why could a man cancel a woman's vow? The answer lies in the family structure of ancient Israel. The head of the household was responsible for the family's resources. If a daughter or wife made a vow that would create hardship for the whole family—promising something they couldn't afford—the father or husband had the option to void it immediately.

Notice that a widow or divorced woman was fully responsible for her own vows. No one could cancel them for her because no one had authority over her decisions.

The deeper principle is this: words matter. Promises to God are binding. Don't make vows carelessly, and don't break the ones you make.

WAR AGAINST MIDIAN

Chapter 31 records a sobering event: war against Midian. Remember the Baal-Peor disaster from chapter 25? The Midianites had followed Balaam's advice to seduce Israel into sexual immorality and idol worship. Twenty-four thousand Israelites died in the resulting plague. Now God commanded Israel to execute judgment on Midian.

Twelve thousand Israelite soldiers (a thousand from each tribe) went to battle. They killed the Midianite kings and warriors, including Balaam himself, the prophet who had blessed Israel but then advised their enemies how to destroy them from within.

The text records in detail how the spoils were divided: half to the soldiers, half to the community, with portions set aside for the Levites and offerings to the Lord. Even captured goods were purified before being brought into the camp.

This is difficult material. The violence is real. But the text makes clear that this wasn't random conquest—it was God's judgment executed through Israel. The Midianites had deliberately attacked Israel through seduction, trying to break their relationship with God. They succeeded partially, and thousands of Israelites died. Now they faced consequences for that attack.

THE TRANSJORDAN TRIBES

Chapter 32 tells the story of the Transjordan tribes. The tribes of Reuben and Gad owned massive herds of livestock. As Israel approached the Jordan, they noticed that the land east of the river—the territory they had already conquered from Sihon and Og—was excellent grazing country. They came to Moses with a request: "Give us this land as our possession. Do not make us cross the Jordan."

Moses' reaction was fierce: "Shall your countrymen go to war while you sit here?" He reminded them of Kadesh, forty years earlier, when the unfaithful scouts discouraged the people and doomed a generation. Was this new generation about to repeat the same mistake?

Reuben and Gad quickly clarified: they weren't abandoning Israel. They would build cities for their families and pens for their flocks on the east side, but their fighting men would cross the Jordan and help conquer the land for everyone else. They wouldn't return home until every tribe had received its inheritance.

Moses accepted this arrangement, with a warning: "If you fail to do this, you will be sinning against the LORD; and you may be sure that your sin will find you out."

Half the tribe of Manasseh also chose land east of the Jordan. So two and a half tribes would settle outside the Promised Land proper—still part of Israel, but living across the river.

THE TRAVEL LOG AND BOUNDARIES

Chapter 33 provides a travel log, a summary of everywhere Israel had camped during the forty years from Egypt to Moab. It reads like a list of place names, most of them unfamiliar to us. But for Israel, these were memory markers. Each location held stories: miracles witnessed, lessons learned, people buried.

The chapter also contains instructions for when they enter the land: drive out the inhabitants, destroy their idols and high places, and take possession of what God is giving them. If they fail to do this completely, the remaining peoples "will become barbs in your eyes and thorns in your sides."

Chapter 34 defines the boundaries of the Promised Land and names the leaders who will help Joshua and Eleazar divide the territory among the tribes.

LEVITICAL CITIES AND CITIES OF REFUGE

Chapter 35 addresses the Levites and the cities of refuge. Since the Levites were set apart for service at the tabernacle, they didn't receive a large tribal territory like the others. Instead, they received forty-eight towns scattered throughout all the tribal territories, along with pasturelands for their livestock. This arrangement spread the Levites throughout the nation, positioning them to teach God's law everywhere. Six of these Levitical cities had a special function: they were cities of refuge.

Here's the problem they solved: in ancient culture, if someone killed another person, the victim's family had the right to pursue and kill the killer. This was called "blood vengeance," and the family member who carried it out was called the "avenger of blood." But what if the killing was accidental? What if someone died in a construction accident, or was struck by a tool that slipped from someone's hand? Was the same punishment appropriate?

God's answer was the cities of refuge. If someone killed another person accidentally (without hatred or premeditation), they could flee to one of these six cities. There they would be safe from the avenger of blood until they could receive a fair trial. If the elders determined that the killing was truly accidental, the person could live safely in the city of refuge until the high priest died. After that, they could return home without fear of vengeance.

But if the killing was intentional—if it was murder—no refuge applied. Murderers must be executed. The land itself was considered "polluted" by unpunished bloodshed, and only the blood of the murderer could cleanse it.

This system accomplished several things at once: it protected the innocent from hasty revenge, it ensured due process through a trial, and it maintained justice for murder victims. The cities of refuge pointed forward to something greater—a place of safety for those who need protection from the consequences of their actions. Christians have seen in these cities a picture of Christ himself, our ultimate refuge.

ZELOPHEHAD'S DAUGHTERS: THE FINAL RULING

Back in chapter 27, Zelophehad's daughters had successfully argued for the right to inherit their father's land since he had no sons. God ruled in their favor and established a new precedent.

But now a complication arose. The leaders of Manasseh's tribe realized that if the daughters married men from other tribes, their land would transfer to those tribes. Over time, Manasseh would shrink while other tribes grew.

Their concern was brought to Moses, and God provided a solution: daughters who inherited land must marry within their own tribe. The land stays in the tribe. The inheritance is protected.

The book notes that Zelophehad's daughters did exactly this—they married their cousins, keeping the land in the family. The ruling showed that while God cared about justice for individuals, he also cared about the community structure. Both mattered. Both needed protection.

WHAT THIS MEANS FOR US

First, rhythms of worship keep God central in ordinary life. Israel's calendar wasn't just about religious holidays; it was about structuring all of life around God. We need similar rhythms: daily prayer and Scripture, weekly worship, regular times of celebration and remembrance. Without intentional patterns, God gets pushed to the margins of busy lives.

Second, words matter—especially promises to God. Making vows was serious because God takes our words seriously. Jesus later said, "Let your 'Yes' be 'Yes,' and your 'No,'

'No'" (Matthew 5:37). We shouldn't make promises we can't keep, and we should keep the ones we make.

Third, there are always consequences for attacking God's people. Midian tried to destroy Israel through seduction rather than warfare. It partially worked, but Midian eventually faced judgment. Those who harm God's people may seem to succeed for a time, but God keeps accounts.

Fourth, commitment to community matters. Reuben and Gad could have abandoned the other tribes and settled comfortably on the east side of the Jordan. Instead, they committed to help their brothers before enjoying their own inheritance. We don't get to skip the hard work of helping others just because our own situation is comfortable.

Fifth, God provides refuge for those who need it. The cities of refuge protected people from unfair vengeance while maintaining justice for genuine crimes. This balance of mercy and justice points us toward Christ, who offers refuge to sinners while satisfying the demands of justice through his own sacrifice.

TALKING POINTS

1. **Israel's worship calendar structured daily, weekly, monthly, and yearly rhythms around God.** What rhythms of worship exist in your life? What might be missing?

2. **The chapter on vows emphasizes that promises to God must be kept.** Why do you think words and commitments are so important to God? How careful are you about the promises you make?

3. **Reuben and Gad wanted to settle east of the Jordan but committed to help the other tribes first.** What does this

teach us about balancing personal interests with responsibility to our community?

4. **The cities of refuge protected people from unfair vengeance while still maintaining justice.** How does this balance of mercy and justice reflect God's character? How does it point to Jesus?

5. **Numbers ends with Israel poised to enter the Promised Land—a journey that took forty years because of unbelief.** What lessons from this book do you think are most important for Israel to remember as they finally cross the Jordan?

LOOKING BACK, LOOKING FORWARD

Numbers began with a census of warriors, organized camps, and a nation preparing to march toward their inheritance. It ends with another census, detailed preparations, and that same nation—now a new generation—finally ready to cross the Jordan.

In between came rebellion, plague, judgment, and grace. Moses himself fell short and would die before entering the land. Aaron died. Miriam died. An entire generation died. But God's promise never died. Caleb and Joshua, the two faithful scouts, were still standing. The children of the rebels were about to receive what their parents forfeited.

The wilderness was never the destination. It was always about what lay beyond: a land flowing with milk and honey, where God would dwell among his people, where they could finally rest.

The book of Deuteronomy will record Moses' final speeches to this new generation. The book of Joshua will tell how they crossed the Jordan and took the land. But Numbers reminds us of everything that happened between Egypt and Canaan—all the failures, all the grace, all the times God remained faithful when his people weren't.

That's the message of Numbers: God keeps his promises. Even when we fail. Even when it takes longer than it should. Even when a whole generation falls away. His purposes will not be stopped.

The wilderness ends. The Promised Land awaits.

www.ingramcontent.com/pod-product-compliance
Ingram Content Group UK Ltd.
Pitfield, Milton Keynes, MK11 3LW, UK
UKHW020420250726
13967UKWH00007B/2737

9 781971 767130